Pitching The Dream

PITCHING THE DREAM

Cheryl D. Lyons

Library of Congress Number: 2004099306
ISBN : Hardcover 1-4134-7751-8
Softcover 1-4134-7750-X

This book was printed in the United States of America.

To order additional copies of this book, contact:
Xlibris Corporation
1-888-795-4274
www.Xlibris.com
Orders@Xlibris.com
25841

January 30, 1925 - April 27, 2000

You compete with yourself and no one else.

- Brooks Lawrence

Acknowledgments

I would like to extend heartfelt thanks to the memory of my maternal uncle, Brooks Lawrence, for providing research materials and photographs, for building bridges so that others could dream, and also to my family, especially my mother Lily (Maidie), my aunt Jeanne, and my uncle Milton for their insight and support.

Most gracious thanks to my mentor, Mrs. Jane L. Ball for her sincere dedication in proofreading and editing in the preparation of this literary work.

A sincere thanks to Bill Dennison at 700 WLW Radio Station, Cincinnati, Ohio, and to John Clark and John Howard for their time and assistance.

Many thanks to all who may read this book.

Epitaph

Baseball is a way of life. It is a way of thinking. You learn discipline, fairness, how to share, how to live together, you learn truthfulness, you learn how to be supportive, and you learn how to depend on someone. If you learn all of these things, it becomes a way of life and spills over all other aspects of your life.

Life is a challenge because it gives you something to look forward to, something to meet everyday, and something to compete in everyday because you compete with yourself and no one else. And life is fun because God gave me life and said, "Here son, do the best you can with it."

- Brooks Lawrence

1st Inning

It was early evening June 21, 1954. A perfect night for baseball in Kansas City. Brooks Lawrence, a 208 pound, six-foot-tall handsome brown-skinned man, was waiting for the game to start. As he stood in the bullpen rotating his right arm his manager, John Keane of the minor league Columbus, Ohio, Redbirds, strolled up to him.

"You won't be pitching tonight," Johnny said, a strangely sad yet envious expression on his face.

"Really?" Brooks said, frowning with disappointment.

"That's right," Johnny said. "I just got a call from the St. Louis Cardinals. They want you to pitch for their ball club day after tomorrow in Pittsburgh."

Brooks' eyes widened and his mouth spread into a surprised grin. He could hardly believe it! He had made the majors! He rushed to a phone to call his father, who had been so supportive over the years and who dearly loved baseball.

When his father's voice said, "Hello?" Brooks blurted, "Dad, I'm going to the major leagues!" Excitement made him sound boyish, almost giddy.

His father was speechless. Brooks knew his dad was stunned, just as he had been when he got the news. After a brief silence, his father said, "The majors?"

"Yeah, the majors," Brooks replied. "The St. Louis Cardinals. They want me to pitch for them day after tomorrow in Pittsburgh."

Brooks could tell that his father didn't know what to say to this fulfillment of a years-old-dream; he didn't know what to say either. Yet, he knew that in his own quiet way, his dad was very proud of him. Brooks told him he would call him later and hung up.

Smiling, he thought, *"I made it. It's a dream come true."* He stared out at the ball field where his Redbird teammates were warming up for the night's game. *"How did I come this far on my journey?"* His thoughts drifted to the beginning of the path . . . .

It was the year 1925, the year Babe Ruth hit twenty-five home runs; Josephine Baker made her debut in Paris. It was the year another star appeared, whose light would some day guide others to follow their dreams.

It was the year Brooks was born on January 30th at home on Linn Street in Springfield, Ohio, to Wilbur and Patsie Walker Lawrence. There were altogether six children in the Lawrence household: His sister Anne was the oldest. Next was his brother Milton, his sisters Lenda and Lily Mae (called Maidie), himself, and his baby sister, Jeanne. He never knew his sister Lenda, who died a year after his parents moved to Ohio. There was also a half-brother named James, born to the union of Brook's father and his first wife, Pinky, who died while James was an infant. James was raised by his maternal grandparents who lived in a town in Georgia.

Brooks' parents had been sharecroppers in Sparta, Georgia. Patsie, brown-complexioned and five feet seven inches tall, she had dark brown hair, which she always wore in a hair net. Except when she went to church—when Sunday arrived, she'd wear her one fancy hat, which accented her finest dress. A usually soft-spoken and compassionate woman, she knew when to be gentle and when to be firm. She had a sixth grade education and could read and write. At night, she would sit by an oil lamp or the fireplace and read to her own mother, Melinda Reed-Walker. Brooks' dad, however, didn't have much opportunity to go to school; he had to work in the fields to help support his family. He could barely read or even write his name, but he had a photographic memory. A handsome brown-skinned man with short black hair and a small, neatly trimmed mustache, he got his high cheek-bones from his mother's side of the family: His mother, Mary, was half Seminole Indian. He was six-one with a large athletic frame, and he walked with a proud straight stride. Brooks always thought that if the strength of a tiger could ever be portrayed, one could see it in his father.

In the Winter of 1922, they had very little money because most of the crops had failed. Feeling there had to be a better way to survive in this world, they finally came to a decision. Patsie wrote to her brother, Willie Walker, who lived in Springfield, Ohio. He wrote back that if they would just leave Sparta, they could do better in Springfield. There was plenty of construction work there and Wilbur could surely get a job. Brooks' parents, being very spiritual, prayed over the idea and decided to make the move. Their parents and brothers and sisters thought they had taken leave of their senses. Wilbur's father, Jule Lawrence, even said to Patsie, "You'll never see that young man again because he's going up North and he's gonna freeze to death!"

The day Wilbur left for Ohio, he wore a white shirt and bib-overalls. He carried a small straw suitcase with a couple changes of clothes and a shoe box filled with fried chicken, biscuits, and fruit. He also carried, unseen but most definitely a part of his baggage, his faith in God that he was doing the right thing. As he walked the dirt road from their home heading for the train station some miles away in Sparta, Patsie waved and watched until he was out of sight. Wilbur had no watch yet managed to get to the train station two hours before the train left for Ohio.

Wilbur arrived in Springfield without enough money to take a taxi to his brother-in-law Willie's house. He asked a Black station attendant how to get there. Either the station attendant gave good directions or God was with him, or perhaps both, because Wilbur walked all the way to Willie's house without getting lost.

Wilbur moved into a spare room in Willie's house and got a construction job the following week. After working a week on the building of the Masonic Home, he got paid and thought he was rich! He had never seen so much money before in his life. Right away he sent some to Patsie, and within a couple of months, she and the children were able to move to Springfield. They all stayed at Willie's house at first, but after a few weeks, Wilbur and Patsie had saved enough money to rent the house next door.

Wilbur was earning enough so that Patsie didn't have to work outside the home after the move to Ohio. Her tasks were the daily household chores, going to the market, paying the bills, and taking care of their kids. Sometimes, she would also take care of friends and neighbors who were ill.

Over the years, their relatives from Georgia came to visit. Wilbur's mother even stayed with them for awhile. Both Patsie and Wilbur came from very large families: Patsie had eleven brothers and sisters, and Wilbur had twelve; and most of their brothers and sisters had quite a few off-spring. A few of the relatives decided to reside in the Springfield vicinity while others chose to stay in the South. Patsie and Wilbur didn't visit the South very often; but every now and then, they would send a care package to a brother or sister whose family was in need. Patsie often said it would take six months to visit all of the relatives just in the state of Georgia, and there would be Lawrences and Walkers until Gabriel blew his trumpet.

The Lawrence family came from a long line of forebears who cherished dignity, pride, and the strength to overcome adversities. Brooks could recall his mother, Patsie, speaking about her lineage. Her dad Charlie Walker's "word was his bond." Everybody respected him, and Brooks' mom was crazy about him. Charlie's father, Pete, had been a slave. A lot of slaves kept their owner's name when they were set free, but Grandpa Pete was not fond of Ole Massa Harris. So when the slaves were set free, he took the last name Walker. Grandpa Pete's right hand was crippled from the severe treatment he received as a slave, so as a free and grown man, Grandpa Pete couldn't do manual work. Instead, he tended to the grandchildren.

Grandpa Pete couldn't read, but he encouraged Brooks' mother, his granddaughter, to learn to read.

When a young man, Brooks often reflected on his parents' quest, like pioneers, to the North. He admired their courage and inner strength to leave their families and friends and venture into the unknown. His mother once told him that her mother would get up every morning and ask all of the children what they had dreamed. After each child responded, she would interpret the dream. Brooks sometimes wondered if the journey North had been one of his mother's dreams. Neither one of his parents had "book smarts". But, when Brooks got older he realized that they didn't need "book smarts" because they had "Mother Wit" and a strong faith in God.

After residing on Piqua Place and then Linn Street, Patsie and Wilbur were finally able to buy a home on West Washington Street which is actually an inclined alley running parallel to the New York Central Railroad track. The Lawrence home was a grey, wooden two-story. It had a large screened-in front porch where family and friends congregated on warm evenings. Its partially cemented cellar, with its cold rock walls, had the chill of an ancient cave. But the small cozy dining area, which was the center room and the warmest in the house, is where everyone gathered during the fall and winter months. An upright coal-and wood-burning stove in the dining room generated enough heat to warm the entire house. Special guests such as the preacher and church deacons were ushered into the parlor with its comforting fireplace while the dining table was prepared for the Sunday afternoon meal. Outside, a huge maple tree dominated the front yard which was surrounded by a wire fence with a latch gate, and every year Wilbur would make a rope swing for the children to play on.

Brooks' parents brought their penchant for farming up North. They cultivated a plentiful vegetable garden, apple and peach trees, blackberry bushes, and a grape arbor. They raised chickens and even slaughtered their own hogs.

The cordial warmth of the homestead was enjoyed not only by the Lawrence family. The home soon became a half-way house for many escapees fleeing the deprivations of Sparta, and the

Lawrences never refused to assist a single one. When they showed up at the front door, Wilbur and Patsie extended their hospitality. Usually, the man of the family would come North first, stay at the Lawrence home, find a job, and then send for the rest of his family. The Lawrence homeplace greeted relatives, neighbors, friends, and even strangers. It was nicknamed "The Traveler's Rest". Even hobos knew the Lawrence home was a friendship house where they could get at least one good meal. Brooks' mother always had cooked food on the stove, even during the Great Depression. Though many a day while growing up, Wilbur, went without a meal, he was always grateful that he could provide a home and food for his family and others in need. The Lawrence house was alive with love and warm memories. It was on West Washington Street where Brooks Lawrence spent most of his childhood and where his parents lived for the rest of their lives.

2nd Inning

When Brooks was born, he was named Ulysses Lawrence, but his parents called him "Brother" and his siblings called him "Little Brother." When Brooks was about five years old, the Bradford kids moved next door. Two of the Bradford boys, Frank, called "Skeeter" from the comic strip character, and John, called "Neck" because he loved neck bones, became his playmates. They, however, refused to call him "Little Brother".

Skeets said, "We're not calling him 'Little Brother'".

"He's not our brother," Neck chimed in.

"That's right," Skeets said. "We're gonna call him something else."

The Bradford boys huddled together to discuss what name to give him.

"We're gonna to call him 'Brooks,'" they finally agreed. "And if anybody asks how did we came up with that name, we'll just tell them it's a secret," Skeets said.

So among his friends and playmates, the Brooks name had stuck by the time he got to fourth grade, though he was still called Ulysses at school.

Early childhood was pretty much a lonely time for Brooks. His sister Anne and brother Milton were much older than he was. His sister Maidie had her own friends, and sister Jeanne was too young. And even though families with children moved in and out of the alley frequently, Brooks played by himself a lot. A favorite game for him was to climb the huge maple tree in the front yard and throw rocks at anything moving or still. He would fill his pockets with rocks and climb the tree to a high limb, where he'd throw rocks or sometimes just watch for his prey.

One day, his mother heard some girls screaming, "Miz Lawrence! Miz Lawrence! Brooks won't let us come up the alley!"

Mrs. Lawrence ran out of the house to find Brooks standing at one end of the alley with rocks in his hand and a pile of them at his feet. He was daring his sister Anne's friends, Jewel and Nettie, to come up the alley.

"You better not throw one!" his mother yelled. "Come on, girls, he won't bother you. Anne's in the house." Ms. Lawrence glanced at Brooks. "You're gonna get it if you're not careful," she warned.

Sulking, Brooks climbed back up the tree. He always seemed to get in trouble. Like the times he tore up Jeanne's and Maidie's dolls to see what made the dolls cry. Or when his mother would call him, and he wouldn't answer. He'd just sit on his tree limb and look down at her.

"You heard me calling you," his mother would say.

Finally, he would reply, "I'm coming,"

But his reluctant compliance was rarely enough to save him from the whipping that awaited him.

He shivered to recall the episode of the frozen sled and the icicle tears: One particularly brisk winter day, his parents warned him that it was too cold to go sledding, but he went anyway. He wore his ragged wool coat, an old beat-up cap with ear flaps, gloves, neck scarf, and boots. He left the house, all bundled up, and trudged through the snow that came up almost to the top of his boots. He walked two blocks over to Light Street hill, and slid down the steep slope for a couple of hours. The chill of winter penetrated every layer of clothes and soon made his whole body tingle painfully with the cold. He came home with tears frozen to his cheeks and his sled stuck to his gloves. His hands and feet prickled like a million needle jabs when his mother dipped them in cool water to prevent frostbite. It took her hand massage and the heat from the coal-and-wood—burning stove to soothe the ache of his stiff, nearly frozen body.

But as he sat in his tree on a warm summer day, thoughts of his past troubles didn't linger long; they melted away with the sun. He knew that he would rather get a whipping any day from his mother than from his father. Although his father was normally a gentle giant, when he threatened to skin Brooks and his brother, Milton, alive, Brooks really believed his father was capable of doing just that. If his dad raised his voice, it would echo like thunder, leaving the Lawrence kids and their friends shaking in their boots. Brooks figured that as long as he didn't have to account to his father for any misdeeds, his luck was still with him.

The Lawrence kids attended Western Grade School. For several years, they were the only Blacks at the school. Brooks entered every grade on conditional status. He would be a B+ student for the first six weeks. After that, lunch and recess were his favorite subjects. He couldn't always go straight home from school when he was in sixth grade because he was always getting detentions. His grade school teacher would make him wait at the classroom corner for at least ten minutes before he was turned loose. He was called a "terror on two feet" because his schoolmates were always pushing him or doing something to exasperate him. However, a ten-minute head start would ensure any kid an escape. Toward the end of each school year, Brooks buckled down and, as usual, would be permitted to enter the next grade. The earlier loneliness phased out of his life when he started school and other kids, especially Bertus, moved to the alley. He and they became known as "the alley rats" to the people in all the surrounding neighborhoods.

One day, a friend of Brooks' parents, named Ms. Charolette, came up from the South. Her husband in Georgia had abandoned her and their son, Bertus. Ms. Charolette, desperately needing a higher-paying job and a better environment to raise her child, decided to venture North. She found a job doing housework and turned over to her in-law, Miz Hat Mammy, the task of taking care of her son Bertus. Miz Hat Mammy was a dear ol' friend of the Lawrence family. She was married to a man named Jack, called "Mr. Jap" by the alley kids, and they had a daughter named Opal. The alley kids didn't like Bertus' name so they nicknamed him "Moose". The alley kids also gave Miz Hat Mammy her name. The name came about because before her grandson Harold was born, she was called Miz Hattie. Harold started calling her "Mammy." The alley kids had nicknamed Harold "Tree Frog" because they said he looked like one. So when the alley kids teased him to make him mad, they would say, "Hat mammy, hat mammy, you got a hat mammy."

"Mammy!" Harold would snap.

"Hat Mammy!" the kids would scream.

After awhile, the name just stuck, and even the adults called her Miz Hat Mammy.

Moose was a few years younger than Brooks, but they became playmates, always tagging each other and running when it was time to go home. One particular time when they were standing at the gate of Brooks' front yard and Brooks didn't realize it was time for Moose to go home, Moose caught him by surprise. He leaned back and tagged Brooks a good one and took off flying around the fence. Brooks saw an old Wilson milk can, and in a flash picked it up and threw it at Moose, who was about one hundred feet away.

Moose looked back with a smirk. He hollered "Addy, addy, addy, I got you!"

Bam! In an instant, the can smacked him on top of his head.

"Wah!" Moose squalled as if someone had tried to kill him. His howl of pain echoed through the whole alley. Neighbors ran out of their homes to see what had happened while Miz Hat Mammy rushed to console Moose. Kids playing in the alley stopped and stared in Brooks' direction. They were astonished!

"He got an arm!" someone said.

"Yeah," someone said. "Throwin' rocks from that maple tree done gave him an arm." As for Brooks, he skedaddled into his house.

The autumn Brooks entered sixth grade, he reached a turning point in his life. An Inner City League for basketball was about to start. He knew that some Keifer Jr. High School students were going to participate, and most definitely students from Snyder Jr. High, a predominantly white school. Brooks dearly wanted to play with the "big boys," so he got busy to earn the fee, which was only a dime. He scrambled for a week, collecting enough iron, rags, tin, and brass to sell to the junkyard at 6 to 7¢ a pound. He was determined to raise the fee to play.

Brooks could hardly wait until Monday, he was so overwhelmed with excitement. When Monday morning finally arrived, he ran all the way to school and burst breathlessly into the principal's office.

"I got my dime!" he exclaimed to Miss Hause, the principal. "Now, I can play intramurals."

Miss Hause stared at him for a few seconds. Then she removed her glasses and lowered her eyes. "I'm sorry, Brooks," she said in a soft German accent, "but I can't take your dime."

"Why not?" he asked.

She adjusted her hair bun and hesitated, "Well, I know you worked hard to earn your dime. But you . . ." she paused, "well, you just can't play."

"I can't play? But the Keifer and Snyder kids get to play."
"You're just not old enough yet," she said, gently.

Brooks stormed out of her office. He cried everyday for almost a week and vowed angrily to get even with "them". He directed his anger toward his schoolwork and got a B+ average through the entire sixth grade.

When the school year came to a close, he thought about what he would do all summer for fun. He soon learned that the City of Springfield was sponsoring sandlot teams, so he decided to try his luck at baseball even though the ball field was five miles away, near the pump house.

One day, while teams were still being organized, Brooks and his friend Bob walked to the ball field and stood on the sidelines watching the different groups practice.

An older teenager on the field looked in Brooks' direction and shouted, "You want to play?"

Brooks nodded and walked over to the guy. "Hi. I'm Brooks," he said.

"My name's Simmy. Can you bat?" he asked.

"I can give it a try," Brooks said.

He grabbed a bat and stepped to the plate. Simmy threw him a fast ball. Brooks took a swing. Only air grazed the bat.

"Strike one!" Simmy yelled, and pitched another fast ball.

Brooks did a repeat.

Simmy held up two fingers on his right hand and said, "That's strike two."

Brooks tried to settle himself, taking some deep breaths. He bunted the next ball, took off for first base, but was tagged out before he could even slide. He looked over at Simmy, shrugged his shoulders and remarked, "I don't do bats."

"Well," Simmy asked, "can you pitch?"

"I can give it a try," Brooks said.

Simmy looked over at the umpire and said, "You call 'em."

Brooks walked over to the pitcher's mound. His eyes dared the first batter-up. With his left leg high, he leaned far back on his right, and spun a fast ball.

"Strike one!" the umpire yelled.

Brooks threw another one.

"Strike two!"

Brooks threw a fast curve ball to deliver the final blow.

"Strike three, batter-out!"

Brooks awaited his next victim, a left-handed batter.

After he hurled three consecutive curve balls, the umpire yelled, "Strike three!"

Simmy was amazed. "Congratulations, kid! You just made pitcher!"

Brooks beamed a satisfied grin. "Thanks."

His friend, Bob, also made the team. So almost everyday thereafter, they both went to the ball field, never noticing how far they had to walk.

The team sponsors gave them T-shirts to play in, labeled "Pump House." Thus, the team became known as "The Pump House Gang." Though Brooks couldn't bat well, he could pitch. He had an arm and eye for it. He could throw balls like he threw those rocks, far and right on target. He knew when he was eight years old that he had an unusual talent. What he didn't know was that one day his talent would become a dream maker. The Pump House Gang was just the beginning.

3rd Inning

R-i-n-g! It was the last bell.

"Late again," Brooks muttered as he raced to the classroom.

It was his first week at J. Warren Keifer Jr. High, and it had been a big adjustment from elementary school. Going to his locker and trying to remember the lock combination, changing classes, different teachers, all done in a matter of minutes, it was like scurrying through a maze.

"You're late, Ulysses," Mrs. Morgan, his geography teacher, said, gazing up from the names in her attendance book.

Brooks, always well mannered, apologized and took his seat.

Mrs. Morgan stood and walked around to the front of her desk. Leaning against it, she looked over her glasses, pursed her lips, and in a high-pitched drawling voice, addressed the class. "Today, class, we're going to study a subtropical tree of Australia. Let your mind wander as you leaf through the pages, and you will discover just how useful the Eucalyptus tree is to mankind."

The students looked over at Brooks and snickered when they started reading about the Eucalyptus tree. After class, a group of boys approached him and said, in a joking manner, "Hey Euke! What's going on, Eucalyptus?" They thought it was funny that Brooks' real name, Ulysses, sounded so much like the Australia tree. The other kids heard them call Brooks "Euke" and it caught like wild fire. Every time he went to his locker or down the hall to class, someone called him "Euke". Brooks knew he had to do something in a hurry to nip this unwanted nickname in the bud. Every time he'd say, "Just call me Brooks," they'd giggle or smirk and go on calling him "Euke" or "Ulysses."

Basketball season saved him. When he made the team, his coach and teammates called him Brooks. After awhile, when he turned out to be a good player, the rest of the school soon followed suit. Years later when Brooks was hired by the Cincinnati Reds Front Office, he and his mother went to the Clark County Health

Department in Springfield, Ohio, and together, officially changed his name from Ulysses to Brooks.

Keifer Jr. High was a training ground that nurtured athletes, a place where boys became men. Excelling in basketball and track, Brooks ran the 100-yard and 200-yard dash relay and the running broad jump for the track team. On the basketball team, he played whatever position needed his skills—center, forward, or guard.

There was only one coach for all the junior high school basketball, track and football teams. Brooks' first memorable coach was Gladden Ronemus, his track and basketball coach in seventh and eighth grade. Gladden, a stocky five-foot-eight man with brown hair, was from the small country town of Moorefield, Ohio. He was great guy and very fair, and being also a farmer he had the patient expectation that everything should be perfect. Since he had never coached basketball before, he read everything about the game in books. And he coached only from the book. But players on his team never had a chance to read the book. So, if the team deviated from the book, the coach was in trouble and totally lost. The games were often wild, with the team running amuck on the court and Ronemus not caring, as long as they won. Keifer Jr. High became city basketball champs during Ronemus' two years at the school. (He went on to Springfield High School to coach track and later to become one of the great coaches in Springfield history.)

Not long after the start of Brooks' first basketball season at Keifer, Ronemus received an unexpected visitor to his office during the last class period of the day.

"Hello, Ronemus," said the tall slender, sandy-haired man standing in the doorway.

Ronemus, puzzled, stared at the man. "Fred Rolfus, is that you?"

"Yeah," Rolfus replied. "It's me."

"Come on in." Ronemus got up from his desk and went to shake his hand. "What brings you here?"

Rolfus got right to the point. "It's that Lawrence kid."

Ronemus felt a twinge of apprehension. "The Lawrence kid? Why, he's one of my best players."

"Yeah, I know. But, Gladden, I have reason to believe he's playing for the wrong team."

"The wrong team?"

"Yes, the wrong team. He's going to a school that's out of his district."

"Really? Well, I'm not so sure about that," Ronemus said. He pulled a city map out of his drawer and spread it across the desktop.

"The boy lives right here," Rolfus said, pointing at a spot on the map. "And that makes him eligible to go to Snyder."

"Well, now if I recall," Ronemus said matter-of-factly, "there haven't been any new district changes in the past several years. So, as I see it, he really lives on the borderline and can go to either school."

"So, o-kay, what are you going to do?" Rolfus asked.

"Well," Ronemus said, "since you brought this concern to my attention, I have to be perfectly honest with you. And I have to be fair to the kid. And the only fair way is to call him down here to the office, and let him tell us which school he wants to attend."

"I believe that's fair," Rolfus said.

Ronemus sent word to Brooks' last period teacher, who sent the boy down to the coach's office.

"Hi, Coach," Brooks said, with a smile hiding his bewilderment.

"Hello, Brooks. I want you to meet Coach Fred Rolfus from Snyder Park Junior High."

Brooks shook the man's hand and said, "Hi".

"Hello, Brooks. It's good to meet you. Your coach and I have been discussing where you live. Did you know that your street is on the borderline of both school districts?"

"No, sir, not really," Brooks replied.

"Well, son," Ronemus interjected, "it looks like you can play either for me or for Coach Rolfus. So I want you to think about which school you really want to be at—We don't have to know today; this time tomorrow will be fine, if that's ok with you?"

"Tomorrow's fine," Brooks said.

"And, by the way," Ronemus said, "you can skip practice tonight, if you want. I'd rather you take all the time you need."

"OK, thanks, Coach," Brooks said. "I'll see you tomorrow."

Brooks walked home from school thinking hard about these new and interesting complications requiring him to make an important decision.

He thought about Snyder Park. If he went there, he would be the only black student in the entire school. He remembered the not-so-pleasant experiences he had when he attended the nearly all-white Western Grade School. The memory was still fresh enough to make Keifer more attractive. Keifer was the school he had chosen in the first place; there were more black students there and he felt more secure at Keifer. And although he knew Snyder Park had some good teams, it wasn't hard to come to a decision. The next day he walked into the Keifer gym after school, dressed for practice. Coach Ronemus smiled with relief. From that day forward, Brooks stayed at Keifer and did well. He maintained a B+ average and lettered in basketball, track, and football.

When Brooks went to ninth grade, his coach was Pete Roberts. Roberts, a big tall man, about six-foot-five and over two hundred pounds, was in his early 20's and fresh out of Miami University of Ohio when he went to Keifer. A Springfield boy, he went back to coach in his hometown. He was not an effective coach, but fortunately he inherited a gifted team with a "world of talent." He really didn't have to do much coaching because the basketball and football players had been well trained to make up their own plays and run them. The track team basically coached themselves and individually worked on delivering outstanding performances. Though Roberts was mostly an ordinary kind of guy who didn't last long as coach, he had sense enough to stay out of the way of his players because the teams usually made him look good.

Roberts had an unpleasant quirk: he got a strange enjoyment out of doing a particular punitive thing to his players. He kept a couple of wooden paddles in his office. When an athlete made what the coach thought was a dumb mistake, he would dish out from five to ten whacks with a paddle, according to what he thought appropriate.

One morning during track season, Brooks passed the coach's office. Coach Roberts caught a glimpse of him and yelled, "Hey, Brooks, come on in here."

Little did Brooks know that what he expected would be a brief pleasant visit would turn disastrous within a moment. The coach lay back in his chair, slapping his left palm with one of the thick paddles. A sneaky boy-grin lit his unusual jovial mood and his eyes glittered with a mischievous twinkle. He stood and sidled over to where Brooks stood.

Still smiling, he asked, "How've things been going?" And without warning, he whacked Brooks' behind with his paddle.

Brooks tightened his muscles to ease the sting of wood. "Ouch!" he said, shocked. "What'd you do that for?"

"Do what?" Roberts joked. "It was nothing."

Brooks' eyes flashed with anger as he exploded with rage. "You've got no business hitting me! I've done nothing to you! You have no reason to hit me! I don't deserve this!" He sputtered with the need to control himself. Glaring, he yelled, "I quit! You hear me? I quit! That's the end of track! I'm done!" And he stormed out of the office.

Coach Roberts hadn't expected Brooks' reaction. He realized he had gone too far with one his better players. He called after him. "Wait, Brooks, I was just playing."

But Brooks kept walking until he had put some distance between himself and Coach Roberts. He simmered angrily throughout the day and avoided going near the gym. He didn't hear from Roberts and didn't want to hear from him. As far as Brooks was concerned, track season was over.

When his last class was over, he went straight home, something he hadn't done in years. He didn't take the short cut, but instead he chose the scenic route. He thought about his agonizing day.

Brooks always stood his ground. Even as a child, he was adamant about the way he felt things should be. He had a definite notion about what was right and wrong. So, his decision about track didn't surprise many of his schoolmates, since the coach's actions had definitely been wrong. But it surprised Coach Roberts. He was floored. Brooks knew what Pete Roberts knew but didn't want to admit: He knew that if Brooks didn't participate in track, the team wasn't going to win. They both knew Brooks was good! He had reached a level of ability where, in a track meet, he could account for twenty points, which meant first place in two or three different events.

A couple of days passed, with neither Brooks nor Roberts giving in to one another. But on the third day, Coach Ronemus got wind of the situation and gave Coach Roberts a phone call.

"Hello, Pete. This is Ronemus. I hear Brooks quit the track team. Is that true?"

"Yeah, it's true. And he's the best kid I got."

"No doubt," Ronemus said.

"I was just playing when I whacked him one," Pete said.

"Well, you should know Brooks doesn't play like that."

Pete's voice was depressed. "What am I going to do?"

"You better talk to the young man. Just go talk to him. He didn't do anything to you. Go get yourself straightened out with him."

"Yeah, o-kay." Pete said. "I'll try. Thanks."

Coach Roberts had Brooks sent to his office. When the youngster came in, the man stood behind his desk and leaned over to face him. "Brooks," he said, sounding sincere, "I'm sorry I gave you a whack with the paddle. I'll never do anything like that again. You didn't deserve that. And if you want to come back on the track team, I'll be more than glad to have you." He waited for Brooks to respond, and the boy hesitated. "What do you say, son?"

Brooks looked into Roberts' eyes with a straightforward maturity. "Well . . . ," he said finally, "I guess I can give it one more try." Coach Roberts smiled. The weight of the likelihood of a bad track season had just been lifted. He could relax in the knowledge that he was back in the running for a winning season.

During one of the next track meets Brooks jumped eighteen feet-10 ½ inches and set a record in Keifer Jr. High track history.

He continued to break records that had been made by his brother Milton, five years his senior. Brooks set records that held until the school closed down in the 1980's.

Six-man football began its first year in the junior high sports program in Springfield when Brooks was in ninth grade. The program, a kind of pilot study, had only a short life span. It was intended to introduce real football to the junior high level, using six players because it would be too hard to put together a high quality team together with eleven players.

Brooks, becoming a well-rounded athlete, tried out for the six-man football team. Because he had an "arm" and could really thread the ball, Brooks made quarterback. That year, the Keifer Jr. High team became city champs with an undefeated season, and the scuttlebutt amongst coaches and townsfolk was that next fall Brooks could start as quarterback at Springfield High School.

Keifer Jr. High played a primary role in Brooks' athletic career. Ninth grade was the year when Brooks put on his game face in preparation for the glitz and glamour of high school sports. Springfield High athletics would require him to be just as good, if not better, demonstrating his discipline and talent, and Brooks looked forward to the challenge.

4th Inning

Springfield High School was the only high school in Springfield during the time that Brooks attended, and was a feeder school for students from five junior high schools. It was primarily all White, with a student body of approximately three thousand, about five hundred being Black students. Because of its enormous size, two graduations were held each year, one in mid-January and one in mid-June. Springfield High, home of the "Wildcats," was noted not just for academics but also for its strong athletic programs. It was renamed Springfield South in the early 1960's after Springfield North was built.

High school was a smooth transition for Brooks. Junior high had prepared him to meet the academic challenges, and he could easily handle class preparation as required. As a sophomore new to the school, he didn't know many students, but the students seemed to know him since he was a rookie star athlete, so he made friends fast.

Jim McDonald, whom everyone called "Mac," was the head football coach. He came to Springfield High for the first time the same day that Brooks started high school. He was a young, tall, dark-haired man whose eyes twinkled when he smiled. He had charisma and personality, and any player would want to model himself after him. He had an excellent athletic background: before coming to Springfield High, he was an All-American from The Ohio State University and had played for the Detroit Lions pro football team.

Bill Stewart, another young man with a great personality, also joined the coaching staff at that time. Fresh out of Miami University (Ohio), he was appointed assistant coach.

When Brooks tried out for and, as expected, made the varsity football team, Mac didn't quite know how to play him. One day after practice, he asked Brooks to stick around so that he could talk to him.

"Brooks," Mac said, "you're quite some player. You have extraordinary and unusual talent. It's rare for a high school coach to see, much less have a player with your athletic ability."

Brooks sat on the bench, patiently listening.

"Well, you know, I was going to play you as either a running back or a fullback. But, the more I watch you practice, the more I see you're a triple threat. You can run, pass, and kick the ball. Besides, I've got some darn good players in those positions already, and I'd like to utilize your talents more." He slapped Brooks on the back. "Amazing," he said. "You never cease to amaze me on the field."

"So, what position do I play?" asked Brooks.

"Well, uh . . ." Mac paused, "I wish I could play you as quarterback, but I don't know if this town is ready for a colored quarterback. You just don't hear of colored high school quarterbacks in predominately White towns. So, I thought I'd have you play tailback. But in reality, you're gonna be the quarterback."

"What do ya mean, Mac?"

"Well, son, you're gonna call all the plays, and tell all the players including the quarterback which way to go and what to do to run the plays."

"I don't know, Mac. What will the guys think? You think they'll go for it?"

"Well, let's try it at practice tomorrow and find out. Okay?"

"Yeah, Mac. Okay."

The practice drill next day was gruesome and rigorous. Mac had devised difficult plays that required precise timing for execution. There was one where Brooks signaled Bob, the quarterback, to hand off the ball to Brooks, who then ran through a hole his teammates created in the center line and then onto open field. This play worked nicely each time the defensive line blocks failed to hold and there was no blitz. After a week of practice, Mac's plan worked.

"As far as we're concerned, you're quarterback," his teammates told Brooks.

By the time Brooks became a junior, it was official that he would be first-string quarterback for the "Wildcats" for the rest of his high school years. The prediction during his ninth grade year at Keifer Jr. High had come true: he became the first Black quarterback at Springfield High School.

The Friday night football games in Springfield, at Evans Stadium, were thrilling for any player, band member, cheerleader or fan. The chants and shouts from the crowd and the drum cadence complemented the school motto, "Spirit and Fight Makes Champs" and added to the game hype. At times competition was stiff for the Wildcats, especially when they played rivals such as Hamilton, Ironton, or Portsmouth high school teams. But when the team experienced an adrenaline rush, no job at home or away was too big for a "Wildcat."

On a crisp night in October 1942, Springfield High played Ironton, after only a couple of weeks of practice. After Herbie, the left halfback, ran a seventy-yard punt return, a whistle shrilled on the playing field and the referee called, "Time-out!" The team huddled on the sideline with their coaches.

"Listen up, guys," Mac said. "We've got to continue to go in there and give it our all. We've got to rush the line and keep running until we get over that goal line. We gotta fight, guys! We gotta fight! Yeah!"

"Okay, guys," Brooks said. "Let's run a draw play. We're going with Sweet Nineteen, Blue Fifty-six."

"Go! Go! Go!" the Wildcats chanted.

They broke their huddle and moved into formation. Brooks looked around to check the team's playing position. Peering out of the corner of his eye to his right, he once again checked the line blockers. It all looked good.

"Hut one! Hut two!" yelled Brooks, "Hut! Hut!"

Jim, the center, snapped the ball. Brooks faked a pass to Bill, the fullback, then handed the ball to Dave, the right halfback, who glided into the end zone. In a matter of seconds, the game was over. Brooks and John, a receiver, had also scored touchdowns that night. The Wildcats defeated Ironton, 29-9.

The Wildcats continued to spank their opposition. They had their first winning season in nine years, since Springfield High won the State Championship in 1933. With Brooks playing forward, the Varsity basketball team also had a winning season for the first time in nine years and won the Greater Ohio Basketball Championship.

But no athletic experience was more gratifying for Brooks than reuniting with the former coach of his junior high days, Gladden Ronemus. The coach had taken Brooks under his wing in those days, training and teaching him how discipline and respect must complement a great athlete. He always had Brooks' best interest at heart, even after he left Keifer Junior High.

Brooks was rushing to class one day, when he bumped into a man strolling along in the crowded hallway. "Excuse me," Brooks said, and took a few more paces before he heard the man say, "Hey, slow down. You're not on the track yet."

The voice sounded familiar. Brooks stopped and turned around. It was Coach Ronemus.

"Hey, Coach," Brooks said, smiling to see the familiar face.

"Hello. Practice starts next week," said Ronemus, almost as though he and Brooks had seen each other just the day before.

"At Evans Stadium?" asked Brooks.

"Yep," answered Ronemus.

"I'll be there," said Brooks. It was beginning to feel like old times, getting back in the routine with his old coach, who was now the coach at Springfield High.

Each day after class, Brooks and his friend and teammate, Johnny, would walk to Evans Stadium for track practice. Brooks ran the 100-yard and 200-yard relays, the hurdles and the running broad jump. Johnny also was a running broad jumper. The team practiced hard with an eye toward winning the championship. Coach Ronemus had high hopes because Brooks and the other boys seem energized and determined on the field. Then one day, Ronemus noticed that Brooks and Johnny seemed a little sluggish. Ronemus walked over to them as they were sprawled out on the field.

"You guys doing all right?" he asked.

"Yeah, Coach," Brooks said. "We're just a little tired."

"A little tired," Johnny echoed.

"We had a bad day at school today. A lot to do, you know. Tomorrow will be a better day," said Brooks.

"Yeah," said Johnny.

But every tomorrow was a little worse. Brooks and Johnny were listless.

"Something's wrong," thought Ronemus. "Maybe I should take them to get checked out at the hospital. I'll wait and see how they do tomorrow."

The next day, Ronemus asked the school nurse if the boys had been to her office, but she hadn't seen them in months. That evening at practice, Ronemus watched Brooks and Johnny. They were sprawled out on the field, again.

"But they don't look sick. They're always joking and laughing. Something's not right. Something must be happening between school and Evans Stadium."

The following day after school, Brooks and Johnny headed off for practice. As they had done for the past several days, they stopped at Miller's Bakery on Liberty Street where their friend Bobby worked after school. As usual, he loaded each of them up with two or three four-inch blueberry and peach nickel pies right from the oven, along with giant sugar and oatmeal cookies. Brooks and Johnny took their usual route through the alleys, so no one would see them munching on their snacks on their way to the stadium.

But this day soon after they had left the bakery, the sound of a car motor hummed behind them in one of the short-cut alleys. Then the car drove up beside them, and the driver rolled down the window.

"Hello, there," he said.

"C-c-coach," they stammered.

Caught, they tried to stuff the rest of their goodies in their pockets.

"So this is what you do before practice," said Ronemus. "Now I know why you're so sluggish. From now on, fellas, you'll be riding to track practice. Get in the car."

Brooks and Johnny got in. They knew they would have to run extra laps around the field, and they also knew that Miller's Bakery was off limits for the rest of track season. Ronemus, always a man of his word, made arrangements for them to have a ride to the stadium for track practice and even for home track meets.

Listening to Coach Ronemus and following his guidance paid off. The team excelled against many of its competitors, both as a team as well as the individual members. The Gold and Blue Wildcats won and held records in relays, placed first in the Southwest District Tournament and captured second place in the State Finals.

Playing sports was challenging and fun for Brooks, but he also found playing the field could be just as thrilling. Girls flocked around all the high school "jocks," and many swooned over him. Though Brooks never thought that he was, in his words, the "cat's meow," he definitely enjoyed the attention of his fans. One young lady in particular soon stole his heart, the beautiful Larcenia Winston. Five-feet-four inches tall, Larcenia, called Dolly, was small framed and pecan brown, with dark brown hair worn in a medium-length bob. She was poor, like most of the Blacks in town, but she had a million-dollar smile and a fascinating beauty mark on her right cheek. She had a classy air and was a brilliant student. Like most of the girls in town, she knew of Brooks Lawrence, but the summer of her sophomore year, she really got to know him. He was a year older, and he and her brother Harold, who was nicknamed "Squirrely," played on a summer baseball league team.

One afternoon, Brooks stopped by the Winston house to pick up Squirrely. They were going to walk to practice together.

As Squirrely ran out of the house to meet Brooks, Dolly stood at the screen door looking at them.

"I'm ready, man," said Squirrely. "Let's go."

Brooks, who could not help noticing the pretty girl, nodded his head toward Dolly, his manner asking the question, "Who's that?"

"Oh," whispered Squirrely. "That's my little sister."

"Wow!" Brooks said.

"Hey, Dolly," Squirrely called. "This is Brooks."

Dolly came out of the house.

"Hi, Dolly," Brooks said.

"I know who you are," Dolly replied, her eyes fastened on his.

Brooks winked at her. "Tell me what do ya know?" he flirted.

Dolly put her hands on her hips trying to act affronted even though she couldn't help being pleased at his obvious interest. "Aren't you supposed to be going somewhere?" she asked.

"As a matter of fact, I am," said Brooks. "Friday night. Center Street YMCA dance. I thought you'd like to join me."

Dolly winked at him and grinned encouragingly. And then she said, drily, "Well, you thought wrong."

"Ahh, come on, Dolly. It'll be a lot of fun. What'd ya say, girl?"

Squirrely, bored, started walking away from the house; Brooks waited for Dolly to answer. Coyly, she turned around and sauntered toward the screen door. After a few steps, she turned around quickly with hands on hips and strolled back toward him. For a brief moment she looked down at her bare feet, her toes rubbing the dirt in the grassless yard. Then she looked straight into his eyes, crossed her arms and cocked her head to one side.

"Friday night?" she said. "Huh."

"Well," Brooks said, as if it was settled.

"Well, what?" She sounded a little indignant, recognizing the sound of victory in that "Well." "Are you gonna talk about yourself?"

"No." Brooks tried to sound less sure of himself.

"Are you gonna think that you know everything?"

"No. I'll pick you up at eight."

"At eight? Who says I'm going?"

"You're going." He knew now that she'd go with him.

Dolly's heart fluttered. *The* Brooks Lawrence, asking her for a date. She thought she was going to melt. Even if she didn't want him to know it.

Brooks winked at her and flashed a smile before racing to catch up with Squirrely. He glanced to see her smile, which lingered even after he was out of sight.

When Friday night came, he and Dolly went to the dance. She was stunning, dressed in an A-line dress that showed off her well-put figure. Brooks was proud to have such a pretty girl on his arm, and Dolly clutched on to him for dear life, feeling part of something much bigger than herself. When they entered the "Y," all eyes were on them. Brooks, sensing her uneasiness, whisked her to the dance floor, put his arms around her, and did a skillful fox trot while the band played a smooth Duke Ellington arrangement. They danced practically every dance.

Afterwards, holding hands, they slowly walked back to the Winston house under the moonlit sky. They talked about school, events of the day, and even recited poetry to one another. They knew that their personalities complemented each other. At her door, Brooks asked if he could kiss her "goodnight." Dolly said nothing but closed her eyes. Brooks leaned forward, aimed carefully, and planted a warm, tender kiss on her lips. He felt sparks of emotion whirling through his body. There was a sweet tingle that made him want to kiss longer. But he pulled away and taking a step backward, he smiled and blew her a kiss "goodnight." Dolly sighed and whispered, "Goodnight." Even though Brooks had not come right out and asked her to be his girl, he knew then that she was, and she knew it, too. For the rest of his high school days and hers, their romance endured and flourished. She would be his girl for years to come.

During Brooks' senior year, Blacks still weren't allowed to play "America's favorite pastime" at Springfield High, but Brooks and some of his friends changed that with a dare and raw talent. Watching the baseball team practice one day, Brooks and his friends stood on the sidelines laughing at them.

"You guys are sorry," they bragged. "We can beat ya with our eyes closed. We could throw a glove at ya'll and win."

The baseball coach, Russ Paugh, heard them and said, "You guys think you're great?"

"Yeah," they said.

"Well, I don't think you're that great. So, put up or shut up."

Eager to take the challenge, Brooks and his friends got a team together, and the very next day met the Wildcats on the baseball diamond. Brooks pitched. By the time they got to the last inning, the score was 15-2, in favor of Brooks' team. Brooks, with his game face still on, walked to the pitcher's mound.

"Play ball!" yelled the umpire.

Brooks pitched two strikes, one right behind the other. The batter scowled, looking determined not to be struck out, no matter what. Egging the batter and then nodding to his catcher that the pitch call was what he wanted, Brooks set his mind to pitch the third strike. He raised his left knee up slowly until it was even with his waist in his usual stance. Then quickly lowering it, he lunged forward, firing a ball that whooshed through the air like a flash of lightning.

"Strike three!" the umpire yelled. The batter's mouth dropped open in stunned surprise.

The game was over. The Wildcats had been stomped by Brooks Lawrence and his friends.

"We told you guys you're sorry," Brooks and his teammates said, trying not to sound too triumphant.

Coach Paugh and his team couldn't believe what they'd seen.

"That's some pitch you got," said Coach Paugh. "How would you like to be on the team?"

"I run track," Brooks said.

"Yeah, I know. But we need a guy like you."

"The track schedule probably conflicts with the baseball schedule."

"I'm sure it does. But I'll tell you what, you can be on the team if you agree to pitch the championship game."

"No other game?"

"No. Just the championship. That way there'll be no conflicts to worry about, and the way you pitch, it can guarantee a win."

"Okay," Brooks said.

So Brooks and three of his friends made the baseball team. But Coach Paugh hadn't considered that it would take a lot more than just having Brooks for one game for his team to become champs. The team never made it to the championship game.

But Brooks lettered in every other sport he participated in and was even all-state honorable mention in football. He was the ultimate athlete.

By his junior year, the United States had declared war on Japan, and gasoline and lots of other things were rationed. But in spite of shortages the high school continued to produce championship teams and the Wildcats still found the means to travel to away games. Many of the athletes began leaving school to join the Armed Services. Brooks' favorite coaches, Gladden Ronemus and Jim McDonald, left for active duty as officers in the United States Navy.

In 1943, two years after the war had begun, Brooks turned eighteen in January. Though his marching orders were deferred for six months, he knew exactly where he would be going within a month after his June graduation. Destination? Central Pacific-Asiatic Theatre Battles and Campaigns.

5th Inning

Guam, the southernmost island in the Pacific Marianas Island chain located between Pearl Harbor and the Philippines, was strategic for the American forces. Closer to Japan than other sites held by the Allies, it was vital for the United States fleet and carrier forces. It had fallen to the Japanese early in the war, but finally after fierce fighting, it was recaptured by the Americans in August 1944. Almost immediately construction began on major airstrips, roads, bridges, and buildings, and Guam soon became one of the most important military installations in the Pacific.

After arriving at "The Pearl" (Pearl Harbor), the Pacific embarkation and training point, Brooks was soon on his way to Guam within a couple of months of the reconquest, to help in the construction of the base. It would be the one and only tour, but a memorable one, he would serve while in the Armed Forces.

His boot camp at Fort Benjamin Harrison, Indiana, had been rigorous. Brooks, already in good physical shape, toughened up even more and learned how to handle himself in extreme conditions. It was there that he met Louis, a soldier who would be his comrade throughout the war. Louis was a tall, thin, brown-skinned former high school star basketball player. He came from a large family of ten, and like so many others, he was pocket poor. But he had a good heart and endearing spirit that Brooks felt comfortable with.

After boot camp, it seemed, all the Black inductees from the North went South and all those from the South went North. It was a time when all of the services were segregated. After a few weeks of basic training, Brooks' outfit was sent first to Mississippi, then South Carolina, and finally to Florida, the staging area for men for overseas tours of duty. From Florida, they took a train to Seattle, Washington, and then caught a boat to Hawaii. Brooks and Louis arrived at the Pearl on June 16, 1944, and on October 1st of the same year, left for Guam, which was considered one of the nicer islands. But it was nothing like the lofty barracks in Seattle and Pearl Harbor.

One morning Brooks and others from his platoon of Army Engineers Aviation Battalion and some Naval Seabees were working on the airfield. It was hot and steamy even though splashes of pink sunrise still shimmered through clouds and reflected off the crystal blue waters. Brooks took a cigarette break, leaning against a supply truck and wiping sweat from his forehead with a limp handkerchief. "It's a hot one already," he said to his comrade Louis. He shook his handkerchief, almost soaking wet from sweat.

"You can say that again," Louis growled. He took a long drag on his cigarette. He exhaled and began to cough, his eyes bulging with the effort.

Brooks glanced at him, "What's wrong, man?" Then he straightened suddenly; he thought he heard a humming sound. His eyes narrowed as he listened and cocked his head.

Just as Louis, who had also heard the sound, exclaimed, "Bandits!" Brooks wheeled about to look up toward the northwest to see the Red Sun rising like a malignant wasp from behind the jungle treetops.

"Attack! Attack!" he shouted the alarm.

Sirens immediately sounded. All the men, who moments before had been going through the motions of the hot tedious work, scattered like frantic bees for cover. Within seconds, bullets were chipping at the ground and everything else, as the Japanese fighter plane began strafing every ground target in sight.

Brooks stopped in his tracks for only a shocked moment before leaping into action. He dashed a few yards to where an artillery jeep was parked. Its mounted machine gun was loaded and ready for action. He jumped into the back behind the gun and grabbed the two grips. Swinging the gun around, he aimed at the enemy plane making its second sweep of the airfield. Keeping the plane in his sights, he squeezed off a volley of shots even as the enemy bullets came perilously close to the jeep. The plane veered off, as if out of control. Brooks was sure his bullets had reached their mark.

The plane began to sputter and a plume of smoke trailed from the fuselage. Within seconds it swerved crazily and, suddenly, dove into the sea.

Brooks released his grip on the machine gun and squinted toward the sky. He stood up and listened for more planes. After a few seconds of blessed silence, he exhaled with relief and jumped off of the jeep to go look for Louis.

Louis crawled out from under the supply truck where he'd taken cover. His face was flushed; he was obviously shaken by the close call. But when he rose to his feet it was apparent that he was not hurt.

Brooks called out to him and he answered in a shaky voice, "I'm o-k-a-y! I'm o-k-a-y!"

All around, the other men were coming out of their havens. A few had injuries from the actual bullets and from flying fragments of everything the bullets had hit and shattered. But there were no fatalities. The men looked at each other as if checking to assure themselves of their escape from disaster. Someone drove up in an army truck to take the men back to camp and the infirmary.

Brooks and Louis helped the wounded into the truck and then climbed in. They lit cigarettes with shaking hands and tried to look nonchalant.

One of the men sitting across from Brooks looked at him, and after a moment, he simply said, "You saved our lives . . . . Thanks."

Realizing how close they had come to death, the other men murmured "Thanks." They knew it was due in large part to Brooks that they had survived.

Brooks, still in shock at his close call and his unexpected daring, just nodded his head and smoked his cigarette. His eyes were hollow as he stared out the back of the truck at the empty sky.

The truck soon parked beside the infirmary and dropped off the wounded. Brooks had a strange case of residual jitters that made him feel the need to get away from the other men. He trotted down the dirt road to the encampment where his pup tent was set up. He crawled inside, rolled out his sleeping bag and lay down. Laying on his back with legs crossed, he folded his hands behind his head and looked unseeing at the canvas overhead. Some rain stains caught his eye and he stared at them, thinking, How did I end up in this snake pit of a jungle?

How indeed. The stains gave him no answer though he stared at them until his eyelids grew heavy. The excitement of the attack, the adrenaline rush as he shot at the Japanese plane, the constantly growing awareness of how narrow his escape from injury or death had been—it drained him. He closed his eyes at last and fell into an exhausted sleep . . . .

. . . All of the family was there. Everyone wanted to give him a good send off. His mother, Patsie, cooked the kind of breakfast guaranteed to stick to his ribs for a good long time and in his memory for always: cheese and eggs, rice, homemade sausage patties spicy with sage, biscuits to eat with sweet butter and sorghum molasses, and grapefruit. She intended that her child, heading off to God only knew where and for how long, would have at least one more decent meal before settling for Army rations. The family hugged him and the women folk plied him with kisses and tears as they said their goodbyes. They were proud of him, going off to fight in the war, but they hated to see him go off to what was certain danger and uncertain outcome.

Byron, his sister Anne's husband, was the only family member who owned an automobile. He finally dragged Brooks away from the farewells; Brooks had a train to catch. At the train station, Brooks and Byron said their goodbyes; Byron had received a last minute deferment because he was an airplane mechanic at Wright Patterson Air Force Base in nearby Dayton. As a civilian, he was already important to the war effort. The two men hugged one last time before Brooks boarded with several other young men on their way to war.

Sitting in a railroad car with a bunch of unknown recruits, the young men laughed and talked; some played cards to pass the time. Once in awhile Brooks leaned his head against the window, gazing at the passing landscape, seeing only the images in his mind's eye.

One image in particular kept coming back to him. His family and his friends and the coaches who meant so much to him were all woven in his thoughts. But like silver thread in black fabric, the image that stood out in his mind was of the flame of his heart, Dolly.

It had been only a couple of nights before that they said their goodbyes. He had to tell her of his impending departure. Her eyes filled with tears almost as soon as the words left his mouth. She managed to say, "I'm going to miss you, Brooks," as the tears streamed to her lips. She wiped a hand across her eyes, trying to be brave.

"Don't cry, Dolly," he said. "I'll be home soon." He gently brushed his lips across one of her weeping eyes, then the other. She leaned into his arms, and tenderly, he kissed her cheeks, her nose, then her lips.

"I'm going to miss you, too," he whispered back.

"Promise to write me?"

"I promise," he said in a somber tone . . .

. . . "Wake up, Brooks." Louis called, sticking his head into the pup tent.

Brooks slowly opened his eyes. Lying still, he stared at Louis. The reality of Guam flooded back to him.

"You got to get up, man," Louis said. "The doc's been asking about you."

Brooks sat up, stretched and scratched his head. Why would the doctor want to see him?

"Meet me at the mess tent," he said to Louis and took off down a dirt path to the dispensary.

The hospital tents were usually filled with soldiers suffering from an unpleasant foot fungus known as "jungle rot." It rained a lot in Guam, and when it wasn't raining, it was very hot. The men didn't get to bathe often, and their sweaty feet, encased in government issued boots would set up an infection. Today was no different from most—more than ten soldiers lay or sat on the hospital cots, passing the time with card games and old magazines.

Brooks stopped at the entrance of the Red Cross tent. When he saw the doctor, he immediately stood at attention and waited.

"At ease, Sergeant," the Captain said. "I'm Doc Hyatt; you must be Brooks."

"Yes, sir. With all due respect, sir, why do you need to see me? I'm not sick. As a matter of fact, I feel fine."

"Well, Sergeant, you certainly don't look sick, but I'd like to examine you anyway. I heard you had a big morning. There's been quite a bit of talk about you." His tired eyes roamed over Brooks' face, carefully measuring his manner.

"It was nothing, sir. Not really." Brooks said, as he took off his shirt before sitting in the nearby chair.

Doctor Hyatt took the stethoscope hung about his neck and listened to Brooks' chest. He tapped and peered and listened for several minutes. After the physical examination he said, "You seem to be in good shape."

Brooks said nothing, as he patiently waited to be dismissed.

"That was a brave job you did today," the doctor continued. "It takes a lot of courage to act quickly and do something like that. Um, you want to talk about it?"

"Not really, sir. I didn't do any more than any other soldier would have done."

"Oh, yes, you did! You saved all the guys. They're grateful. And your commander is very proud of you, Sergeant, and I am, too." Feeling that Brooks might need to "release," the doctor continued, "If you ever feel that you want to talk about this morning, you know where to find me."

"Thanks, Captain." Brooks stood up to salute the army doctor and then left to meet Louis.

Louis was standing by the mess tent and spotted Brooks coming from the infirmary. When Brooks reached where he was standing, Louis asked what the doctor wanted.

Brooks grinned. “He said that I was in good shape.”

“Did you tell him about this morning?

“Nope. He wanted to know about it, though.” Brooks shrugged. “I guess he wanted to hear it from my lips since he heard it from everybody else. Maybe he thought you all left something out. But I didn’t say nothing.”

“You didn’t say nothing? Why not man? You’re a hero.”

“Uhn uhn. No way. I’m really trying to forget about it. I didn’t do nothing.—Anyway,” Brooks took out his mess kit, “let’s eat. I’m starving.”

They walked into the tent, and stood in the shortest dinner line. All three coal-oil stoves had a pot of beans on them. When they got to the serving station, with their mess kits at the ready, the cook dished out a huge helping of beans. Brooks and Louis found a couple of wooden crates outside near the mess tent and sat down to eat. To take some of the gloom off the dull meal, they talked about high school and sports and never once mentioned the events of the morning.

After dinner, one of the men in the outfit needed Louis’ expertise to repair a short wave radio—Louis liked to tinker and was handy. When he left with the soldier, Brooks walked down to the beach. The ocean made him feel that he was in another realm where nothing else really mattered, and the fresh salty air seemed to purify him. The waves had a way of soothing the day’s drama, and all events of the day faded with the sunset. It became a therapeutic survival tactic for him. Sometimes he would take to the beach the letters he received that day from Dolly or his family. He missed home and just wanted this job to be over with soon.

Occasionally, he got a reminder of home when someone from Springfield was stationed at Guam. One time an old friend, Clark, sought him out after reading of his whereabouts in a Springfield Center Street YMCA bi-monthly newsletter called *The Informer*. The newsletter contained notes on servicemen, letters from servicemen, names of those who got inducted, or got discharged, those who didn’t make it back, furloughs, changes of address, and community stuff. Mossey, the editor of the paper, would send copies to the servicemen.

One late afternoon, while Brooks was walking towards the beach, an army jeep pulled alongside of him. The soldier driving at the wheel beeped the horn. Brooks looked dumbfounded. At first, he didn't recall the dark brown face shaded under the army cap, but when the soldier shouted his name, he instantly recognized the deep raspy voice. Clark jumped off the jeep and embraced him. It felt good to Brooks to see someone from home.

Since Clark was first sergeant and got a few privileges, he often procured a jeep and drove around to different companies looking for someone from home. So far on the island, he had found only Brooks. But not too long ago, on one of the other Marianas islands, he found a guy, from Brooks' neighborhood.

"What job they got you on?" asked Clark.

"Building airfields. What about you?"

"My company hauls supplies with the amphibious trucks."

"The Ducks?"

"Yeah. We just pull up beside a supply ship that's out in the middle of the ocean, load up, and make drop-off runs to some of the other islands."

"So you guys must be getting some of the best supplies for your company?"

"You better know it," Clark said. "We steal the best. We eat like the colonels and generals. Sometimes we bring our home folks or other fellas from nearby camps to our company, and feed them or give them supplies. We've made a lot of friendships with companies we associate with. We even have all the smokes and beer we want."

"Just beer?" asked Brooks.

"Yeah," Clark said. "Just beer. Usually a captain or major is riding the ducks with us, so they take all the whiskey." They chuckled and both lit cigarettes.

Clark's talk about the supplies he got was making Brooks hungry. He imagined the mouthwatering meals that Clark's company devoured everyday. He hadn't eaten that good since his "last supper" at his parents' house.

"You ever get caught?" asked Brooks.

"No," Clark said. "But we came real close once. One morning, when we were unloading the supply ship, the colonel got off the ship to ride back with us. Man, were we nervous? He wanted to check our mess tent. We only had some ground beef, so that didn't bother him. He had bigger worries. Evidently, there was a lot of meat missing, and they weren't eating too swell, so he was going to have to check some other companies. Everybody's stealing!"

Clark looked at his watch and when he noticed it was almost suppertime, he asked Brooks if he wanted to join him. Brooks flashed a wide grin and leaped into the jeep. He knew that whatever he ate, it was going to be better than eating at his camp's mess hall. He licked his lips all the way to the campsite. At mealtime they had steak with mash potatoes and gravy.

After supper, Clark dropped Brooks off at his camp. Brooks didn't tell anyone where he had been. He just wore a little smile the rest of the night.

During the two years he served in the armed forces, Brooks played baseball every chance he could. It became a favorite recreation and pastime. At first, he just played at his leisure with some of the men in his company. But on Guam, he played with one of the army teams, consisting of men from different companies on the island. When the entire Marianas islands chain had finally been secured by the Armed Forces in the Spring of 1945, these teams would fly to the different islands to play ball games.

One day when some of the baseball teams were enroute to play in Iwo Jima, Brooks noticed that he and another soldier were the only two black men on the plane. That evening, on the way back to Guam, Brooks made a point to stand beside the black soldier before boarding the plane. The soldier's name was Jim Pendleton and he was a utility infielder. They chatted a few minutes before boarding the plane, then went their separate ways.

Neither Brooks nor Jim knew that friendship lay ahead for them in the future. And neither knew that playing baseball in the service would frame their future professional careers.

In early May 1945, Germany surrendered. Many of the troops who successfully fought the Nazis were sent to storm the Pacific Theatre to finish the job against the Japanese. After the second atomic bomb was dropped on the city of Nagasaki, Japan, on August 9, 1945, the Japanese surrendered. Within a month, they withdrew their forces from Southeast Asia and the Southwest Pacific, and the war was finally over. The men of the American armed services, though eager to go home, were kept at the task of rebuilding the islands and territories that were severely damaged by the war. Still they hoped to get back to the States by Christmas.

Brooks wrote to his sister Maidie that he might be home for Christmas. When she replied, she enclosed a self-addressed post card and told him he was to drop it in the mail before boarding the ship for home.

On December 1, 1945, Brooks dropped the post card in the mail and headed for home. He went back first to Pearl Harbor, then to the state of Washington. But he didn't make it home for Christmas day: on the morning of December 26, he and his comrade Louis were sitting in a room with seventy other soldiers in the Separation Center at Camp Atterbury, Indiana. They were attending a small ceremony where some of the men would be given medals they had earned. All would receive their honorable discharge papers.

An officer, Major Frizzelle, stood at the podium slowly calling out the names of the medal recipients in a slow monotone. Brooks was antsy—he wanted the major to hurry up so that he could get his papers and get out of there.

After a few names were called, the major said, "Sergeant Brooks Lawrence."

Brooks, not really listening, didn't budge.

Louis nudged him. "Man, that's you," he said.

"What do you mean, that's me?" Brooks asked.

"That's you." Louis repeated. "You got a Bronze Star."

Brooks walked reluctantly to the podium where Major Frizzelle pinned the Bronze Star Victory Medal with its service ribbon onto Brooks' uniform. Wordlessly, Brooks went back to his seat, and waited for the ceremony to end.

When it was over, he leaned over to Louis and said, "I'll see you outside." He went back up to the podium where the major stood gathering up his papers.

Major Frizzelle looked up with surprise to see him standing there.

"Excuse me, sir." Brooks said. "I don't think I earned this medal."

Major Frizzelle frowned! "Why not?" he asked, shuffling through the papers. He didn't think he'd made a mistake.

Brooks waited silently until the major found what he was looking for.

Major Frizzelle found Brooks' name on the list. "Oh, yes, you do," he said, and pointed to the paper. "See? Your name is on here for meritorious service in the Central Pacific Asiatic Theatre battles and campaigns."

Brooks looked at the list. It clearly said "Sergeant Brooks Lawrence." Dumbfounded at this unexpected turn of events, he managed to salute and say "Thank you, sir," and walk briskly out of the room.

Louis was waiting for him in front of the building smoking. "What did you do, man?" he asked.

"Not much." Brooks said and lit a cigarette.

"I see you still got your medal."

Brooks raised his eyebrows as if perplexed. They smoked in silence until the army buses arrived to take them to the train and bus stations.

Brooks and Louis embraced, realizing that though they were finally about to see their loved ones once more, they might never see one another again.

"Well, looks like we're free," Brooks said.

"Freedom," said Louis.

They began to laugh.

"I'll try to write," said Louis.

"Me, too." said Brooks. He grabbed Louis' hand and shook it. Then they went to board different buses.

The men on Brooks' bus cheered and sang all the way to the train station. In a few hours they would be home. Even though a day late, still, a perfect Christmas gift.

Photographs, courtesy of Brooks Lawrence

Brooks and Cincinnati Reds' teammate, Frank Robinson.

Brooks sharing a moment with Columbus, Ohio
Redbirds' Bill Greason and Company.

Members of Cincinnati Reds on the 1956 All-Star team.

Brooks hurling a fastball for the Cincinnati Reds (1956).

Brooks and Harvey Haddix.

Caribbean Champs for Caguas team (1953-1954).

Brooks playing for Cincinnati Redlegs.

Members of Cincinnati Reds on the 1956 All-Star team in dugout.

Brooks on Cincinnati Redlegs team (1957).

Brooks and his wife, Dolly.

Brooks holding baseball after pitching a "two-hitter" against the Brooklyn Dodgers at Ebbets Field (1956).

Brooks and Ken Griffey Sr.

Brooks on Springfield High School's varsity basketball team during his senior year.

Brooks, George Crowe, Joe Black, and Frank Robinson.

1972 CINCINNATI REDS ORGANIZATION MEETING

SEPTEMBER 18-20, 1972 RIVERFRONT STADIUM CINCINNATI, OHIO

Brooks and other members of Reds Front Office (1972).

Brooks as a pitcher for the Zainesville,
Ohio Indians (1949).

Brooks and John F. Kennedy.

Brooks greeting John F. Kennedy during his
Presidential Campaign stop in Springfield, Ohio.

Brooks in pitching formation (1956).

Brooks on St. Louis Cardinals team (1954).

Brooks as a quarterback for
Springfield High School's Varsity football team.

Brooks as a rookie pitcher for the St. Louis Cardinals (1954).

6th Inning

Brooks was twenty-one years old when he left the service. He left the war where it was and talked very little about his experience. For the most part, in conversation he might utter, "You have no idea how people have to live." The way people lived in the Third World left a profound impact on him, but the drama of the war itself he considered just an inevitable phase of his life, and now he was more than ready to step into a new role. He had never really had a real job before he was drafted; and now that the war was over, he had no idea what he was going to do. Knowing that he could not live at home without having a job, he soon found work at National Supply Company, making engines. It was hard work, but he was strong. The pay was good, between 70 cents and $1.00 an hour, but he didn't like manual labor. After working at the factory for almost a year, he weighed his options: The army had shown him a different world, and he knew there could be something better somewhere with a future of possibilities. He was determined to find it.

He decided to take advantage of the GI Bill of Rights and get a college education. He didn't want to go to a "Big Ten" school, nor did he want to attend a college too close to home. He had kept in touch with his high school coaches, Gladden Ronemus and Jim McDonald, and told them of his plans. They both recommended Miami University, a public school in southwestern Ohio, about seventy-five miles away from his home. The university was small and noted for academics. It also had good sports programs. After a brief visit, he applied and was accepted for admission. In 1947 he enrolled for the winter semester at Miami University. He chose to major in physical education, despite his love of Greek mythology and both classic and contemporary literature. He enjoyed campus life and the college town of Oxford. He roomed with three other Black guys. Sometimes they would go to Brooks' home for the weekend, and his mother would prepare a feast for the poor, starving college boys. He still loved baseball more than anything and tried out for Miami's baseball team, making pitcher.

When school was out, he worked construction with his father and also played summer baseball for the Springfield Tigers, though this was against Miami's rules. Yet, no one questioned his eligibility because the Tigers weren't considered semi-pro or professional league baseball.

During Brooks' second season with Miami, he pitched three wins out of four games. By the time he played summer baseball again, he was pitching really well. One day after a Tigers' practice, Ned, one of his teammates, approached him on the playing field.

"Man, you get better each season," Ned said, admiringly.

Brooks tossed the ball back and forth in his mitt. "It's just been two," he said, ignoring the compliment.

Ned leaned against his ball bat and asked, "You ever think about playing for the majors?"

Brooks raised his eyebrows in disbelief. "The majors?" he repeated.

"Yeah. What's wrong with that? You're good enough, you know."

"Good enough? Says who?"

"Coach and the rest of us. Oh, and the newspapers, of course."

"Well, they haven't said nothing to me. Besides, you have to make the minors, first," Brooks said, walking away.

Ned grinned. "They will," he said. "You'll see."

Brooks stopped walking when he heard Ned say, "They're having try-outs in September, you know. You really should think about it, man, especially now that Jackie Robinson's broken the color line."

The mention of the miracle of Jackie Robinson breaking into the major leagues, playing for the Brooklyn Dodgers, sent a chill down his spine. It made him wonder if he really could have a chance at the majors.

He slowly walked on off the field pondering his brief mound experience. So far for the season, he had pitched eighteen wins with only three losses for the Tigers. His 8 wins-no losses Army record also came to his mind. He looked around the field, tossed his ball high in the air and caught it. Gazing up at the sky, he smiled. "Maybe I could have a chance," he nodded. "Now that Jackie's opened the door. Maybe I could."

In the stadium locker room, his coach and other teammates were standing around, some dressing, some just talking. When Brooks came in, they drifted toward him, everyone talking at once. Time after time he heard Ned's words about minor league try-outs and someday playing for the majors. Brooks was good at hearing only what he wanted to and heard one voice loud and clear: His coach said, "It's a three day try-out, September 10th, 11th and 12th. Just think about it, Brooks. Think about it."

Early Friday morning of the following week, he rode thirty miles to Dayton, Ohio, with Ned and a couple of other teammates to try out for the Dayton Indians, of the Class-A Central League. Several other eager young men joined him that morning to try their luck for a position with the Cleveland Indians farm club.

The try-outs were long and rigorous; only an occasional breeze cooled the hot dust of the playing field. But Brooks was ready for them. He met each day fresh, mentally and physically prepared for the grueling challenge. Hoping to secure a hurler position, the right-handed pitcher threw curve balls and fast balls with the instincts of a natural.

By the second day of try-outs, some of the cockier guys bragged that they'd be going to Spring training camp in Florida. The others just tried to stay focused on their exposition. Brooks, with his usual calm manner, stayed even minded and silently prayed for a hurler's position. On Sunday, when his last try-out was done, he waited on the pitcher's mound for the decision. Looking toward the third base foul line, Brooks overheard Hank Gowdy talking to Joe Vosmik, the Dayton manager, and another man. Gowdy was a Cleveland Indians scout who just the day before had given Brooks some valuable pointers.

"He's got some talent," Hank said to the man.

"You bet he does," Joe responded. "How much do you think he'll want?"

"I don't know," the man said. "Probably a lot."

The three men looked over at Brooks, whose face revealed his curiosity. Joe called out to him, "Sure, you got a chance."

"Thanks!" Brooks said with a huge smile. He whipped off his ball cap and wiped the sweat from his face. Without another word he left the mound and headed for the dug out. Hank called out to him.

"Hey Brooks, I need to see you for a minute."

Brooks trotted over to where the men were standing.

"I'd like you to meet Eddie Stumpf," said Hank. "Eddie is Cleveland's Business Director, and of course you already know Joe."

Brooks shook Eddie's hand.

"We want to offer you a contract," Joe said.

"How much do you have in mind?" Eddie added, expecting Brooks to ask for a substantial bonus.

"The money doesn't matter so much," Brooks said. "I just want to play baseball, and I'm thankful to the Cleveland organization for giving me a chance."

The minor leagues are a major contributor to the development of a ball player's talent. It is where players learn the ins and outs of the game and how to meet the tremendous challenge of getting to the top. It usually takes three years to become good enough for the major leagues. The talented flamboyant Negro Leagues, organized since 1920 due to segregation, produced seasoned players such as Jackie Robinson, Larry Doby, Roy Campanella, and a few others who made the majors. But usually players of high caliber from the Negro Leagues were too old to spend years in the minors before reaching for the majors. So, the path of Black ball players in the future appeared to lie with young Black ball players such as Willie Mays and Hank Aaron, jumping into the majors from the minors. Yet, even if age or race weren't factors, it's tough getting through the ranks of the minor leagues, and most men don't make it.

Brooks was twenty-three years old when he made the minors. He decided he would give "this baseball thing" a try and if he didn't make the majors in five years, he would just go back home, get a factory job, and complete his college degree at night. He felt comfortable with this decision, knowing he could always go back to the same place he left. Within a week, Eddie Stumpf signed Brooks to a Class-A contract. Brooks withdrew from college at the end of the 1948 fall term and worked construction with his dad. In March 1949, he was on his way to Florida for spring training camp.

When Brooks arrived at the camp, he was amazed that the Indians' farm system was so large and consisted of teams from states other than Ohio and Indiana. (Over the next few years there were quite a few Black players at Spring Training Camp, and some of them, like "Sad" Sam Jones, [named after the original "Sad Sam Jones,"] David Taylor "Davey" Hoskins and Harry Leon "Suitcase" Simpson, went on to play for the majors and made a place in baseball history.) The Class-A Dayton Indians assigned Brooks to the Class-D Zanesville Indians. Not only was he the first and only Black player on the team, as he had been with Miami, he was the first and only Black ball player in 1949 in the entire Ohio-Indiana League. Yet, the D-League was the lowest on the totem pole. It was going to be a long haul for Brooks to reach the ultimate goal of all ball players . . . the major leagues.

Brooks played all of his games in Ohio during his first year with the Zanesville Indians. His debut game was a smashing success. It was a sell-out crowd in Municipal Stadium against the Richmond Robins, and Brooks pitched a three-hitter, fanning ten and walking only two players. Though the end result was impressive, the game got off to a shaky start with Brooks giving up three hits and one run in the first inning. It took a while for the Z-Indians to catch on fire, but once they did, smoke signals went up and sparks flew. In the bottom of the fifth inning, the Z-Indians trailed 1-0, until one of their players led off with a walk and ended up on second base due to the catcher sacrificing him. After that play, Brooks was up to bat. Positioning himself, he watched the pitcher, hoping to read the signal. Bending forward, the Robins' pitcher slightly hesitated while deciding what to throw. He suddenly delivered the pitch and Brooks, a right-handed batter, swung at the fastball as it sped across the plate.

"Strike One!" the umpire yelled.

Closely eyeing the pitcher's body language, Brooks suspected that there wouldn't be a curve ball. Once again, the pitcher threw a fastball, but this time Brooks connected and drove a long fly ball to the right field corner. Making a hard run to get the ball, the Robins' right field catcher fell down, and the second baseman scored. Standing on their feet, the crowd roared their delight. The Indians' centerfielder, Johnny, came to bat. He drove short and Brooks scored. Johnny ran to second base as the Robins' shortstop threw the ball wildly past first.

The seventh inning was equally exciting as the fifth. The clapping of hands and stomping of feet rumbled like thunder through the bleachers when Brooks went up to bat. The Z-Indians had one out. Determined not to make it two outs, Brooks doubled to right center. After Johnny batted a single, a right fielder named Ridgley went to bat and singled Brooks home again. By the end of the ninth, the Z-Indians had clobbered the Richmond Robins by a score of 5-1.

Brooks spent one season with the Zanesville Indians. The following year, 1950, he was sent to the Pittsfield, Massachusetts, Indians to play Class-C ball in the Canadian American League. He had a good year with Pittsfield, and the next season, he was sent to Harrisburg, Pennsylvania, to play Class-B ball. Near the end of the season, the team was going to dissolve and no longer be a part of the Interstate League, so Brooks was transferred to Class-A Indians ball in Wilkes-Barre, Pennsylvania, to finish out the season. He was a favorite with his fans and, on August 16, 1951, the Harrisburg Senators Black Booster Club hosted an Appreciation Night for him at Island Park. The governor of Pennsylvania, John S. Fine, sent him a Western Union telegram expressing "best wishes" and an apology for not being able to attend the event. The governor also said, "Baseball knows no race, no creed, no color, no party. Sportsmanship is the basis. It is great to be honored by the devotees of such sport." The governor's message and the loyalty of the fans touched Brooks' heart deeply. After Brooks finished the season with the Wilkes-Barre Indians, he went home.

The following year, 1952, the team became the Redding, Pennsylvania Indians and remained in the Class-A League. In June of 1953, because the Cleveland Indians didn't have any room for him on their roster, they traded him to the Portsmouth, Virginia, Merrimacs in the Piedmont League. This meant he would be playing Class-B ball again. He felt his career was now going backwards, and this really frustrated Brooks. He had climbed up from the low spot of the totem pole, and suddenly playing Class-A ball wasn't good enough. It wasn't because he lacked youth and talent, but because of the times and how things were. He couldn't change the color of his skin. He couldn't change the way some men thought. But he could change his career path, and he intended to do just that as soon as the season ended.

Playing that year with the Merrimacs, Brooks had a sizzling baseball season. He pitched eighteen wins and hoped for a shoo-in to reach the coveted mark of twenty. But when a rival team withdrew from the league leaving a schedule blank, there were only one or two more games, instead of seven, to try to accomplish the difficult feat. Still Brooks became a leading pitcher in the Piedmont League and was selected to play on the All-Star team. Nevertheless, he planned to stick with his decision to quit baseball, find a job, and earn an honest living.

As fate would have it, his plans would take a detour.

One morning, after Brooks had returned home from the 1953 season, he got a call from Mickey Owen, a major league catcher who also managed the Winter League Caguas ball club. The winter, off-season for baseball is from October through February, and during that time Winter League ball clubs play in the Caribbean Classics and Latin America Series. Brooks didn't know that finishing the season with the Piedmont League, he would give Mickey Owen the chance to discover his talents.

Brooks headed out the back door to walk over to a friend's house when the phone rang and his mother answered it. Hurrying to the door, she called to him as he neared the railroad tracks. "Brooks!" she yelled. "Come back, you've got a phone call. Someone named Mr. Owen."

Brooks stopped and looked back. “Tell him I’m not here,” he said.

“It sounds pretty important, son. It’s about baseball.”

“Why is he calling me,” Brooks muttered. “I’m done with baseball.”

He went back to the house reluctantly and picked up the phone. “Hello.”

“Good morning, Brooks. This is Mickey Owen with the Caguas ball club. How are you this morning?”

“Fine,” Brooks said drily.

“I’ve been watching you play with Portsmouth this year, and you’re quite a talented ball player.”

Brooks interrupted, “Excuse me, Mr. Owen, but, sir, I’m done with baseball. I gave it a shot and now I gotta make an honest living and get on with my life.”

Flabbergasted, Mickey said, “What do you mean, you’re done with baseball? Do you know how gifted you are?”

The sincerity in the man’s voice was so unexpected, Brooks was taken aback for a moment. He said, “You think so?”

“I know so. Come play for me in the Winter League. You won’t regret it.”

His dream of becoming a major league player came back to him, but he hesitated. “Well, I don’t know, sir.”

“It’ll do you a lot of good, Brooks. It’ll help you put things in perspective and you know it’ll be a lot of fun.”

Brooks knew in his heart that Mickey might be right. Maybe he should have one last hoorah.

“When do I report, Mr. Owen?’ asked Brooks.

“Now.” Mickey replied. “Your ticket will be at the airport.”

“Plane ticket, to where?” asked Brooks.

“Puerto Rico. I’ll see you there,” Mickey said, and hung up the phone.

Latin American hospitality and the warm tropical climate melted away Brooks’ resistance to a future in baseball. In Puerto Rico, Mickey made Brooks believe in his dream again. He took the two-pitch hurler in hand, and taught him how to throw a sinker, a slider and a change-up. The team played against a lot of Latin American teams and Brooks pitched with ever increasing skill. In the past, the Caguas always finished at the bottom of the barrel, but this season was different. Class-B pitchers traditionally couldn't win against AA and AAA teams. But Mickey told Brooks that he could win anywhere, and that's just what he did. The Caguas won many decisive victories and even captured the play-off championship in the Caribbean Series. It was the first time the Puerto Rican League had won in nearly twenty years. Brooks tied for the lead amongst Puerto Rican league pitchers and had team support from such great players as Hank Aaron, Charlie Neal, Felix Mantilla, and Chi Chi Olivio.

In 1954, during the winter baseball selection process, Brooks hoped to play with the Cincinnati Reds. Mickey Owen had called the Reds and told them they better get Brooks on their major league roster or they were going to lose him. But Cincinnati, with no room on their major league roster, opted him out to Oklahoma City in the Texas League. The St. Louis Cardinals however, picked Brooks up and signed him to their farm team, the Columbus, Ohio Red Birds of American Association AAA League.

In March 1954, Brooks arrived at the Columbus Red Birds' training camp in Daytona Beach, Florida. Class-AAA ball is considered the best of the minor leagues, and players of this Class are treated accordingly. News reporters were constantly snapping pictures or interviewing the players on and off the field. While at the Red Birds' Daytona Beach camp, Brooks befriended and roomed with Bill Greason, who had been one of the top pitchers of the Class-A Texas League the previous year. Greason, 28, and Brooks, 29, were the first Black men ever carried on the Columbus Red Birds' roster, and they both hoped to be called up to join the mound staff of the parent St. Louis Cardinals. After Spring training camp, Brooks continued to room with Bill, and they became close friends.

At the start of the season, the Cardinals called Bill to pitch. Brooks was happy for him, and Bill with a twinkle in his eyes jokingly said to Brooks, "As soon as you get as good as me, they'll call you." Then on June 21, 1954, just before the start of a game in Kansas City, John Keane, manager of the Red Birds, gave Brooks some breath taking news: The St. Louis Cardinals wanted Brooks to pitch in Pittsburgh. He had finally made it!

While he was in flight going to Pittsburgh, Bill was in flight to Columbus: the Cardinals had sent him back to the minors. Thoughts whirled through Brooks' mind as the plane cruised to its destination. *Did he have what the Cardinals were looking for? Could he deliver?* He didn't know what lay ahead of him, but whatever it was, he knew he would embrace it. He had come too far and wasn't about to let the dream become deferred. He had worked hard and paid his dues. Now, the time had come for him to live the dream.

7th Inning

The rain was pouring when Brooks arrived in Pittsburgh on June 22. He hailed a taxi and headed straight for the hotel where the Cardinals were staying. Eddie Stanky, manager of the Cardinals, was in the hotel lobby to meet him and help him get settled in a room. Stanky, a medium size guy, five-foot-eight inches and not especially muscular, was known among the major league players as "Mugsy" or "The Brat." He had been one of the great ball players of his time and at this point in his career, he had eased from player-manager to just manager for the St. Louis Cardinals. After he took Brooks around, introducing him to his teammates, Stanky handed Brooks a baseball and said, "Start pitching."

Brooks, a perplexed look on his face, watched as Stanky walked out of the hotel. *Surely, he didn't mean that,* he thought. *I just got here. He's just trying to welcome me to the team.* Brooks tossed the ball up and snatched it out of the air. Sure that Stanky was just being friendly, he settled in for the evening.

The next morning was a game day. Brooks was a little nervous, although he tried to dismiss Stanky's last words out of his head. He arrived early at Forbes Field and sized up the stadium. Then he walked to the clubhouse where a catcher named Sarni approached him with a wide grin on his face. "You got your glove?" he asked.

"Yeah. Why?" Brooks said with a curious look in his eyes.

"Oh, didn't you know? You're pitching today."

Brooks gulped. "I'm doing what?"

"You're pitching today," Sarni repeated. "Welcome to the majors."

"Ok," Brooks said, keeping his voice nonchalant. He was trying to seem undaunted in spite of all the butterflies fluttering in his stomach.

His new teammates laughed and joked while they all waited for the rain to stop. But Brooks could only think about the predicament he was in. He had come to play ball, sure, but not on his very first day. He had thought all he'd do today was put on the uniform and sit out this game on the bench. He figured after a couple of practice sessions, maybe then he would be called to pitch. The downpour got heavier and drowned out his thoughts. Puddles filled the players' positions on Forbes Field, and finally the game was called off.

The next day, June 24, 1954, at 2:04 p.m., the twenty-nine year old rookie made his debut in his first major league game. There were 2,637 fans were in attendance that afternoon at Forbes Field, more people than Brooks had ever played for. The butterflies that plagued his stomach the day before began to flutter, but the crowd saw a young man who seemed cool and very calm. Standing on the pitcher's mound, Brooks blocked out the crowd noise to hear only the voices of the second base infielder and the catcher. Before going into his wind-up, he stretched and touched his toes. Then he slowly raised up, with his right foot positioned a few inches forward. Holding both hands above his head, he clasped the ball in his glove. He could hear the voice of his Caguas coach, Mickey Owen, in his head, *You've got a good slider and curve ball, use them. Don't keep them in your pocket.*

He stood on the mound, chewing several sticks of gum and deciding on his pitch. Because of his habit of sticking his tongue out at the corner of his mouth every time he threw a slider, he chewed gum to keep from giving away his favorite weapon. He was motionless, deciding, while the Pirates' batter tried to read the pitch. Then with his left knee bent a few inches above his right one, Brooks quickly did a right angle turn and unleashed a slider ball, a strike the batter didn't see coming. Two more strikes and the batter was out.

In the first four innings the Pirates were scoreless to the Cardinals' three runs. In the fifth inning, the Cardinals scored again, but then the Pirates got lucky, hitting three successive singles to produce one run. The crowd began to rally. The Cardinal's exceptionally good right fielder, "Stan the Man" Musial, approached the pitcher's mound to Brooks' surprise. Being a seasoned major leaguer, Stan wanted to reassure Brooks not to get frustrated because of one run.

Musial smiled, his eyes twinkling. "Now Brooks," he said in a convincing tone. "Calm down. And just remember that it's just another raggedy ballgame."

"Yeah, man. Thanks." Brooks said.

Musial walked back to his position. Brooks stood, with his glove on his right hip. *Well, that's a clever way of looking at it,* he thought, relaxing.

Brooks quickly snuffed the rally. He took a few deep breaths and began to pitch a "no hitter" for the rest of the fifth inning. By the end of the game, the Cardinals won with a score of 5-1. The Pirates lost before the four-hit pitching of Brooks as he set the home team down during the first, third, sixth, seventh and ninth innings. Brooks got rave reviews from the sports writers.

From his first major league game until the end of the season, he did something that hadn't been done in many years: He pitched 159 innings in thirty-five games, winning fifteen while losing only six. He accomplished this feat in little more than half the season. He pitched as often as four days in a row, and for his first thirty-seven days that he was in the major leagues, he was in sixteen ballgames. In this day and age, pitchers are not allowed to be used this much because the owners, league and baseball association will not permit over use of pitchers. But during the era Brooks played, over-pitching was an accepted practice. Once, a sportswriter for the *St. Louis Post-Dispatch* asked Stanky if he thought he was hurting a player if he over-pitched him. Stanky said, "no." But he was desperate and would do whatever it took to have a winning season. Brooks didn't mind because he was having a good time. He proved that he was durable and dependable. He kept himself available in the bullpen between starting assignments, and because of his willingness to either start or relieve every day if necessary, Stanky nicknamed him "The Bull." Sometimes Brooks thought that he was going to pitch a fantastic game and be able to throw even through a brick wall. But his fantasy would last only an inning because the team would get stomped. And there were other times when he would stand on the pitcher's mound, with either his head or his stomach aching, wondering why was he out there. And in spite of the aches, these would be the times he would deliver a marvelous ballgame.

The year 1954 was a year of triumph and struggles. Aside from the emergence of the modern Civil Rights Movement, it was the year the New York Giants' center field star, Willie Mays, became the National League's batting champion and was also voted the league's Most Valuable Player. It was the year that Brooks made the major leagues and was named to *The Sporting News* magazine's 1954 Rookie All-Star team. Being a twenty-nine years old rookie and older than most players, Brooks was at the peak of his maturity and also in his prime. Not only had Mickey Owen developed Brooks into a top-notch pitcher by teaching him different pitches, but he also taught him baseball percentage: Brooks had learned that every batter who has one weakness really has two because you could out guess him by pitching to his batting fault or to his old-strength (As Brooks later described it-"a batter may not be able to handle a ball close to him but can murder the outside pitch. But after you pitch to the inside long enough and back him off the plate, then the outside becomes his weakness and vice versa.")

When Brooks joined the Cardinals, he roomed with another black baseball player, Tom Alston, who was already on the team. Tom was the first black player for the Cardinals and had joined the team at spring training camp in 1954. Tom had an extraordinary talent as a defensive first baseman. But within a month after Brooks arrived, Tom was struggling with his batting stroke and with a thyroid condition. Eventually, he was sent to the minors to play for Rochester (of the International League), and Brooks became the Cardinals' only black ball player for as long as he remained on the team. But he didn't feel like a token because he wasn't treated like one. Black baseball players had to be twice as good as the white players, or they would be gone—the major league would not keep them if they weren't exceptional.

At the time Brooks started with the Cardinals, there were quite a few black players in the major leagues, including such luminaries as Jackie Robinson, Larry Doby, Don Newcombe, Willie Mays, Hank Aaron, Ernie Banks, Gene Baker and Joe Black. Even though the major leaguers didn't earn "mega" bucks, they were expected to wear sports jackets and be presentable at all times. They were celebrities in their own right, and for the most part, Brooks, like many others, was trying to live a glamorous life he knew little about. Society depicted the ball players as entertainers, and many times due to segregation, black ball players stayed at black-owned and operated hotels where they met a lot of black musicians and actors, such as Duke Ellington, Billie Holiday, Sidney Poitier, and Dinah Washington. The black players befriended one another because they really didn't have anyone else to be friends with. If a black ball player was in town for a game, it didn't matter if he didn't know anyone or where to go or what to do because black players of the home team were going to look after him. The black players would meet after the game and go to the best restaurants and entertainment clubs. In this way, black baseball players bonded and were like fraternity brothers.

Though the American version of apartheid was a way of life in the South, Brooks, as a youth growing up in the North, wasn't aware of much difference between blacks and whites because neither he nor his family were ever treated with prejudice in Springfield. Probably this was so because the Depression had equalized things: almost everyone was poor. But by the time he got to high school and played football and other sports, he had a pretty good idea about what a person of color could and could not do. He accepted that he couldn't go into the same restaurants or stay in the same hotels as whites, and he didn't expect otherwise.

As a consequence, he never felt discrimination or segregation. Besides, his high school coaches tried to avoid situations where he would be subjected to unequal treatment.

Brooks had married his high school sweet heart, Dolly, while in the minor leagues and they had two children. Yet, segregation in the minors was just as bad as it was in the majors and very few men, if any, would subject their families to such treatment that they sometimes encountered on road trips, which could last at least three weeks before a two-week home period. However, after Jackie Robinson broke the color line, he had taken care of most of that. But one of the places that Jackie hadn't taken care of was St. Louis, where the most southern team in the league was located during that particular time. The Cardinals' ball club treated Brooks fairly well, but off the playing field, he was sometimes confronted with discrimination. For instance, one time while waiting with his team in a St. Louis train station, Brooks sat with his pitching coach who ordered two drinks, a beer for himself and a coke for Brooks. The waitress glanced at Brooks and then looked at the coach. "I can't serve him," she politely whispered to the coach. In order to get around the embarrassment, the coach said, "Well then, I'll just drink them both." Even when the Brooklyn Dodgers would come to St. Louis, Jackie and his black teammates couldn't stay or dine at the palatial Chase Hotel with the rest of their team. They had to stay at the DeLuxe Hotel in the black section of St. Louis.

Brooks first met Jackie on the ball field. He was thrilled to finally meet his hero when the Brooklyn Dodgers came to town, but at the same time, Brooks heart pounded when he first confronted him on the playing field. He knew that the mind game would intensify as they carefully watched each other's every move. After Brooks threw three balls and two strikes, Jackie stepped away from the plate and took a practice swing. Jackie slowly walked back to the batter's box to take his position. He stared at Brooks as he awaited the pitch. Taking a couple of deep breaths to regain control, Brooks again reminded himself that Jackie was just another player, another opponent. Before Brooks could lean forward bending his left knee to pick the catcher's sign, Stanky suddenly called time-out and burst onto the field running towards the pitcher's mound. A puzzling look covered his face.

"Well, Bull, what do you think?" asked Stanky. His voice was a bit shaky. "Are you going to throw him a fastball?"

"No way," Brooks cooly responded. "You've got to be out of your mind if you think that I'm going to throw him one of them. I've got something special for this guy," he added.

"You do?" Stanky exclaimed.

Brooks winked. "Yep," he said with a reassuring smile. "He's getting a real sweet curve ball with some smoke on it. It's going to be a dandy."

"Okay," Stanky said, nodding his head in approval and then heading to the dugout.

"Play ball!" yelled the umpire.

Brooks took the mound and prepared to throw. His eyes swiftly roaming the field, he found all the infielders awaiting his cue. Brooks started the wind up, reared back hiding the ball, and unleashed a pitch at lightning speed. Jackie swung and missed the ball as it sizzled across the plate.

"Strike three!" the umpire shouted.

The fans cheered and Brooks grinned with a sigh of relief. Walking off the field, Jackie turned and looked at Brooks for a while. His eyes and facial expression flashed a message of warning that was very clear. Brooks instantly knew from that look that whatever he did in future encounters with Jackie at the bat, not to ever throw him that pitch again. He could throw anything else, but not that one because Jackie would never let it pass him by again.

At the end of the game Jackie approached Brooks. "What are you doing after the game?" he asked.

Shrugging his shoulders Brooks replied, "I'm not doing anything. My family is not here."

"Meet me when you leave the clubhouse and we'll go for a walk."

Brooks met Jackie outside the stadium. They walked and talked for a couple of hours, and became good friends for a lifetime. By the end of the 1954 season, not only did the Cardinals surprised him with a $3,000 bonus for a sensational June-September record as a rookie, but Roy Campanella named Brooks to be part of his barnstorming squad. Roy, an outstanding catcher for the Brooklyn Dodgers, had a Black All-Star team consisting of many great players, such as first basemen Monte Irvin of the Giants and Tom Alston of Rochester; second baseman Junior Gilliam of the Dodgers; third baseman Hank Thompson of the Giants; shortstop Jim Pendleton of the Braves; outfielders Larry Doby of the Indians, Minnie Minoso of the White Sox, Bill Bruton of the Braves, and Willie Mays of the Giants; catcher Charlie White of the Giants; and pitchers Don Newcombe of the Dodgers, Bob Trice of Athletics, Joe Black of Montreal, Davey Hoskins of the Indians, and Brooks. Roy also played.

Barnstorming helped ball players earn a few extra dollars after the regular baseball season. No matter how good they were or how much better they did than most, they, like the other players made no money playing ball. Baseball has a minimum and maximum salary scale. St. Louis paid Brooks the minimum salary of $6,000 when he was first signed. In actuality, it cost many of the ball players to play; their families had to support them. The major league black players got paid for what the ball club thought they could do and nothing other than that. In essence, the black players were paid for something that many of them would do for free, and for the most part, that's how the black ball players looked at it. They played for the love of the game. Unlike in the minor leagues, families didn't have to pick up the major league players at the end of their road trips, but most major and minor league players played for the season and then returned home to go to work at another job for several months.

Players enjoyed barnstorming because they were allowed to play any position that they wanted to and got to tour the country. It also gave baseball fans who couldn't attend regular season games an opportunity to watch their heroes play. Campanella's barnstorming tour included game schedules for the continental U.S., Hawaii, the Philippines, Japan, Colombia, Puerto Rico, Panama, and the West Indies. When Brooks first started barnstorming, each player realized around $3,000 after a thirty-one game trip. (But a couple of years after that, the barnstormers were lucky to break even because they would go in on a percentage deal taking eighty per cent of the gate and sometimes they couldn't play due to bad weather.)

A couple of days after Brooks got home from his rookie barnstorm trip, he got up and sat on the side of his bed. He felt that familiar nagging pain in his stomach again. He remembered the couple of times his stomach ached really bad during the regular season. He had gone to a doctor to see what was wrong and what he could take for it, but the doctor politely dismissed him saying, "Now, go on someplace and have a cup of coffee. You'll be all right."

He rubbed his stomach for a moment, his mind on the money he'd made barnstorming and how far it would go to support his family until the season started again. He rose at last and went into the bathroom. He could hear Dolly in the kitchen making coffee and a light breakfast. He wondered if the kids were up.

Suddenly, the pain hit him again, and he thought, *Now that I'm home, maybe I should see a doctor about this, if I don't feel any better soon.* He opened the bathroom door and as he stepped into the hallway, everything went black. He collapsed to the floor.

8th Inning

The dimly lit room didn't look familiar to Brooks as he slowly woke from a deep sleep. Opening his eyes wider, he saw the pretty nurse standing by his bedside changing an I.V. solution. She smiled and said, "Hello."

"Where—?" he whispered.

But she quickly interrupted, "You're in the hospital, Mr. Lawrence, and you're going to be just fine."

"Hospital?" Brooks' voice indicated his confusion.

"Please don't try to talk right now. I'll go get the doctor. He should be in shortly."

Brooks' eyes followed her to the door and then scanned the room. He noticed the blood transfusion drip and wondered what in the world had happened to him. The stomach pain he had felt before had subsided, but when he tried to sit up, weakness overcame him. He closed his eyes and lay still waiting for the doctor.

"Hi, Brooks," Dr. Corbin, his family doctor, said cheerfully as he entered the room. The young doctor was very pleased that his patient seemed to be recovering.

"Hello, Doctor Corbin. Well, I guess I threw myself a curve ball," Brooks joked.

"And luckily it didn't go over the ball park," Dr. Corbin responded.

They both laughed, shaking their heads in agreement. And then they both fell silent. Their eyes met and Brooks solemnly asked, "What happened to me?"

"Well, we're treating you for a bleeding stomach ulcer. All the tests indicate that you've probably been working up an ulcer for the past two years."

"Really?" said Brooks. His mind flashed back to the St. Louis physician who hadn't taken the time to examine him to find out what was wrong. The ulcer was probably bleeding then. "All those times I had a stomach-ache," he continued, "I thought it was just nervousness or something I ate." He pointed to the transfusion drip. "And that thing?"

"You lost quite a bit of blood, Brooks. We had to give you eight pints. Your wife donated that one. It's the last pint."

Brooks smiled. He thought with wry amusement, *They're giving me Dolly's blood. Surely I'll never be in my right mind, ever again.*

"You're a very lucky young man. You got here just in time. A half an hour longer would have been too late."

Grateful that his life had been spared, Brooks whispered, "Thank you."

Dr. Corbin smiled. "Your family is waiting to see you," he said. "I'll give you a few minutes with them and then I want you to rest."

Brooks' illness was serious. Even though he was recuperating, he wasn't out of the woods yet. The St. Louis team officials were extremely concerned about their star rookie's illness and wanted to be kept aware of his condition each day. Under no circumstances did they want to lose their sensational star rookie. Dr. Corbin considered surgery and got second opinions from two young doctors, an internist and Dr. McLemore, a vascular surgeon. If surgery had to be done, the team officials wanted a surgeon whose credentials met their expectations and would send him to Springfield to operate. However after reviewing Dr. McLemore's credentials, the Cardinals' officials agreed that he could perform the surgery. Brooks' doctors and team officials knew that surgery might end his career. Since they didn't want to take that chance, they agreed surgery should be a last resort. Brooks was put on a strict diet of cream, baby food, and all the milk that he could hold. After a few days of this regimen, surgery was no longer an option. His recovery was miraculous.

After final x-rays and a ten-day hospital stay, Brooks was released to go home. His discharge instructions required that he continue his strict diet for the next few months. While recovering at home, Brooks discussed his illness by phone with the Cardinals' club officials to negotiate his 1955 contract and reach salary terms. A few days after Christmas, he welcomed a present from the Cardinals:

They had sent him a contract with a considerable increase over his 1954 salary.

Brooks was the first member of the team to sign for the 1955 season and was ordered to report to spring training camp in St. Petersburg, Florida, on March 1st. When he arrived at camp, he was healthy, looked good and had even gained weight. But he soon discovered that he had a major strike against him: He had no strength. Since his pitching arm was weak and he was easily winded, his stamina was hampered by both slow speed and low agility. He was off to a poor start, and the Cardinals were, too. Eddy Stanky became so agitated with the team that his mood swings got him in serious trouble. The Cardinals fired him early in the season, and his replacement was a man named Harry Walker, who had managed the Rochester minor league team for St. Louis. Walker was from Pascagoula, Mississippi. Before his change of heart in later years, he didn't like anyone or anything black. Since Brooks was the only black player on the team, he knew to stay out of Walker's way. And Walker allowed Brooks to pitch only rarely, mostly in throw-away games.

Since Brooks still hadn't regained his strength and could no longer pitch the kind of commanding games as before, on August 19th Walker sent him and his 3-8 record to Oakland, in the Pacific Coast League, the only minor league he had not played with. Once again, Brooks faced a hard climb to the top. Dismayed at the prospect, and tired of being treated like a piece of meat, he contemplated leaving the baseball profession. His new assignment directed him to go to Oakland and, after the Pacific Coast League's season was over, go back to St. Louis to finish the Cardinals' season. Even though being sent back to the minor leagues was like being jolted by a lightning bolt, Brooks found some good in the Oakland environment. The need to win did not prey on him, and he was able to get his strength back. But more than anything, he could pitch the way he wanted to pitch. He regained his confidence and finished the Oakland's season with a smashing 5-1 record. Then instead of returning to St. Louis when the Pacific Coast League's season was over, he went home.

When Brooks arrived in Springfield, he told Dolly that if the Cardinals called looking for him just tell them that he hadn't got home yet. He needed time to think. Dolly had no problem honoring his request because she really didn't like sharing Brooks with the love of his life. As far as she was concerned, baseball required too much of Brooks' time, and she preferred him to stay at home, get a job there and spend more time with her and the kids. While Brooks took time to figure out which direction his future should take, he pondered the insensitivity of ball clubs. When a player got closer to the top, the game got more challenging and much dirtier. He remembered the intentional spike wound that he got in a minor league game with the Columbus Redbirds, when he ran to cover first base. It had required thirteen stitches in his leg. Yet, he was like the phoenix, he would rise from the ashes. Maybe it was a challenge at the top, but the test for him and other black players was more than just surviving unfair treatment. They were on a mission. They were trailblazers. Jackie Robinson had left the door wide open and they had to keep it open if the younger black players were going to have a chance. Searching for answers, he talked with his father and brother-in-law Byron, who only confirmed what he knew deep in his heart, that he could help keep the door open and make a difference.

For the next couple of days after he got home from Oakland, Dolly intercepted the phone calls from Walker. But on the third day, while she was out for a morning walk, the phone rang and rang. Brooks just stared at the telephone, not sure if he should pick up the receiver. *I might as well get this over with,* he thought and on the tenth ring he finally answered.

"Hello."

"Brooks," a furious Walker growled, "Where have you been? I've been calling you for days! You get back here, right now!" And without letting Brooks answer, Walker slammed down the phone.

Hearing the dial tone, Brooks put the phone back on the receiver. Annoyed with Walker's behavior, he went out on the front porch, to let the fresh air blow away his anger. *I'll get back there all right,* Brooks thought. *But it won't be "right now." You'll see me whenever I get there.* He decided to leave that evening, driving. By September 13th, Brooks had reunited with the Cardinals in Milwaukee to finish the season.

After the season ended, Brooks and his best friend Joe Black visited New York for a few days. Joe was a powerful 6'2" and 220 pounds dark-skinned young man, a graduate of Morgan State University in Baltimore, Maryland. His deep voice rang of friendship and his smile shone with his zealous spirit. He and Brooks first met when he pitched for the Brooklyn Dodgers; now he was playing for Cincinnati. After rooming together while barnstorming earlier that season, the two became like brothers.

While in New York, they ran into the author James T. Farrell. Brooks had met Farrell previously in the St. Louis clubhouse before a game. That day, when someone asked the ball players to list their favorite hobbies and pastimes, Brooks said he liked to shoot pool and read novels and great literary classics. One of the guys in the clubhouse, a little guy named Rice, asked him, "Bull, who wrote the book *Studs Lonigan*?"

"James T. Farrell," Brooks replied.

Rice quickly said, "Just a minute now, I want you to meet Jim Farrell."

Brooks looked in disbelief at the man introduced as James T. Farrell. They talked for a few minutes. Farrell was pleasantly surprised that Brooks had read his book. After this brief meeting, they later became friends.

Farrell had always been impressed with Brooks' intellect and love of literature. So during the course of their conversation in New York, he said, "You know, Brooks, I think you should be on a game show like 'The $64,000 Question.'"

Brooks and Joe burst into laughter. They thought he must be losing his mind.

"Why don't you two come with me?" Farrell continued. "There's someone I want you to see."

Brooks and Joe went with him to an office on Madison Avenue. Farrell knew the woman sitting at the desk. "Hello," he said, "I think I have somebody who ought to be on your show."

"And who might that be?" asked the woman.

Farrell nodded his head towards Brooks and introduced her to Brooks and Joe. Now Brooks and Joe were absolutely positive that Farrell was crazy! But the woman didn't think so. She gave Brooks an inquisitive look, wondering what a baseball player could know about literature. She fired a question at him, "Well, Mr. Lawrence, won't you please tell me who wrote *Captain, My Captain.*"

"James Whitcomb Riley," Brooks fired back and then recited some lines, '"O Captain, My Captain / The fearful trip is done / The ship has weathered every wreck / The prize we sought is won."'

Impressed, the woman asked him about other literary classics and asked a couple of unrelated questions. Brooks accurately responded without hesitation.

"Incredible," she thought. She asked him to leave his address and then said, "We'll get back with you soon."

Brooks and Joe laughed all the way home. They thought the encounter was hilarious and didn't believe in their wildest dream that Brooks would be on a game show. Yet, sure enough, shortly after Brooks returned home, he received a questionnaire with all the questions that he would be asked on the game show. He immediately called Joe.

"Joe, man," said Brooks, "these people are going to have us on the show!"

Joe was excited.

"They just sent me a questionnaire. We're going to be on 'The $64,000 Question'! Boy, we got to do some studying."

"Okay, Bull. We'll get it all figured out; I'll be your guru."

Joe and Brooks started studying, and figured out all the answers, but they weren't sure in what order the questions would be asked or if the game show host would even ask all of the questions. Soon after the New Year, the game show people sent him a note, telling him that he was scheduled to appear around the first of March. But Brooks realized that they couldn't go on the game show at that time because it was the time of spring training. Disappointed, he called Joe and told him of their predicament. They both agreed that it would be in their best interest not to appear. They later found out that they made the right decision because the bottom fell out of "The 64,000 Question." The game show was found to be a fraud and was forced off the air in the face of widespread bad publicity.

However, Brooks had a new issue to contend with. Frank Lane was the new general manager of the Cardinals' ball club. He had a reputation of trading anyone to anybody at anytime, which had earned him the nickname of "Frantic Frankie." Gabe Paul, the shrewd general manager for the Cincinnati Redlegs, gambled on Lane's reputation and made him an offer. He convinced Lane that left-handed pitcher Jackie Collum could solve all of the Cardinals' pitching problems; he would trade him for the Cardinals' Sonny Senerchia, who was also a pitcher, and Brooks. So on January 30, 1956, Gabe Paul called Brooks on his birthday to notify him that the Redlegs had bought his contract.

At first, Brooks was stunned to hear of the trade and somewhat miffed that Lane hadn't even bothered to discuss it with him. Despite his poor showing with the Cardinals, he thought that they would keep him, especially after his 5-1 record with Oakland. After all, their doctors had pronounced him cured from gastric ailments. But obviously they felt no obligation to keep the team integrated and in spite of Brooks' record, they considered him washed up. However, Brooks gradually began to see the trade as a welcomed development. He'd always had a strong desire to play for the Redlegs some day. He grew up listening to the Reds' games on the radio. At ten years old, he had seen his first major league game when his father and Byron, his brother-in-law, took him to Cincinnati to see the Redlegs play. Sitting high at the back of the bleachers to watch the game, he marveled at all of the things he got to see and all of the people there, and thought that it was the greatest thing in the world to be at such a game. Now that the trade was a done deal, Brooks felt he would be right at home playing for the Redlegs, a dream would be fulfilled, and it could be the biggest break in his baseball career.

9th Inning

It was hot in Florida and the heat of the Civil Rights Movement was at its peak, scorching Tampa and most other areas in the South. Brooks felt comfortable in Tampa as a Redleg and settled quickly into the spring training routine. But stepping outside of the Redlegs' spring training camp was like stepping into the twilight zone. Experiencing southern-style segregation brought moments of frustration and disillusionment for Brooks. While he knew very well the problems with segregation in the North, segregation for the "Northern Negro" in the South called for a serious re-adjustment in thinking. In Tampa, there were always two water fountains at the airport, the bus terminal and every other public place, one marked "Colored" and the other marked "White." If there was only one water fountain available, black folks didn't drink. The white ball players could enjoy sandy beaches and world famous restaurants during their leisure time, but these diversions were denied the Black players. They were limited to a few movie houses and one fairly decent restaurant in the Black community of Tampa. Sometimes it was difficult for them to even buy a coke or candy bar. And late at night there were no places for them to buy pizza or hamburgers to appease their hunger pains, although often the white ball players helped out as much as they could. What Brooks saw in the South was appalling.

Brooks was class conscious, identifying himself with other middle and upper class people. He didn't think of himself as being a racist. As far as he was concerned, segregation had always existed within the races. There were white people that he wouldn't go near, and there were black people that he wouldn't even entertain the thought of associating with. Yet, the demonstrations at the downtown lunch counters had little or no effect on him. He didn't want to take anything away from anybody; he only wanted the freedom to choose his own way of life and give his children the best, what he imagined every decent human being wanted.

Cincinnati was slow to integrate its roster after Jackie Robinson broke the color line in 1947. It wasn't until 1954 that third baseman Charles "Chuck" Harmon became the first black player for the Redlegs, and in 1955, Joe Black became their first black pitcher. In 1956 when Brooks joined the team, there were several black ball players on the Redlegs' roster and at the spring training camp, such as his best friend Joe Black, and Chuck Harmon, Patricio "Pat" Scantlebury, Bob "El Mucaro" (The Owl) Thurman, Curt Flood and George Crowe, who joined the team soon after spring training. A young rookie, Frank Robinson was an outfielder and only twenty years old when he made his debut. Just like Hank Aaron and Willie Mays, Frank was much younger than many of the black ball players. Because of the age difference on the Redlegs' team, Brooks, Joe and the other black teammates were less friends than mentors of the young rookie, who stayed with the Redlegs for ten years. (Eventually, Frank was inducted into the Baseball Hall of Fame and also became the first black manager in major league baseball. Curt Flood, who was also a youngster, appeared in only eight major league games and was traded after the 1957 season. Years later, he filed a civil suit against major league baseball, an effort that foreshadowed the free agency option.) Having black teammates was a nice change for Brooks. It also reflected the progress being made for equality in major league baseball. Still, it was a time when there seemed to be a gentleman's agreement in the league that no more than four blacks would be on the playing field at any one time.

Spring training camp perks, such as, the creature comforts of a good hotel, were offered only to the white players. The black ball players had to look for accommodations in the black community. Even during exhibition games in Fort Myers, Sarasota, and other cities outside of Tampa, they were dispatched to some black civilian's house and had to wait in line for the bathroom. Brooks and his black teammates first stayed in a boarding house in Tampa, just as when he lived in St. Louis. But in subsequent years at spring training camp, he and his black teammates had the opportunity to stay with Dr. A.L. Lewis during their six weeks' stay in Tampa. Dr. Lewis was a tall, soft-spoken, middle-aged physician, prominent in the black community. He had a $50,000 home that was located in the slums, and he lived there with his wife and daughter Delores. Dr. Lewis, a native of the South and also educated there, knew the limitations of the South at that point in time. He extended his hospitality to the Redleg delegation to accommodate the black ball players. With his wit and instinct, he was a great host and role model for Brooks and his fellow Black teammates. The guys could shoot pool in the recreation room, enjoy the Lewis' stereo hi-fi record collection of jazz and blues, or eat as much food as they wanted in the well-stocked kitchen. The comforts of his home were comparable to those which the ball players' economic and social status had accustomed them to.

After spring training camp, the Redlegs would leave Tampa and take the train North. On their way back to Ohio, they would get off the train at various places, such as Chattanooga, Tennessee, Greenville, South Carolina and Memphis, Tennessee, and play ballgames all the way back home to Crosley Field, which at that time was the smallest ballpark in the major leagues. One time when the team arrived in Memphis they all got off the train together, and the white players hopped on a bus that took them to a hotel where they could eat, change, and get ready to go to the ballpark that afternoon. The black players were left stranded on the street corner.

"Now, what?" asked Chuck.

"Well," Brooks said calmly, "we'll just have to wait and see if a taxi or something will come by and pick us up."

"Man, this is ridiculous!" snapped Joe. "We got a game this afternoon, and here we are stranded on the street corner like it's no big deal. Management has got to start doing better than this! Gee wiz."

While they stood on the corner, a young black man passed by, and Brooks stopped him. After he quickly explained their predicament to him, the man told him where he could find a restaurant in a nearby black neighborhood. After the man walked away, Brooks spotted a couple of taxis down the street.

"There's a couple of cabs over there," Brooks said. "Maybe we can find the restaurant and a place to change." His teammates looked disgusted.

"But we don't even know if the driver will take our fare," said Chuck. "And we surely don't know where we're going."

"Well, let's get down the street and find out," said Brooks.

They took off running. Brooks and Joe jumped into the first cab, and the driver took their fare up front. Then Chuck and Frank climbed in. The taxi spun off in the direction of the restaurant. The other players had jumped into the second cab. They got to the restaurant, a little greasy spoon with high prices and small portions. And when they finished their meal, they had enough daylight left to search in the neighborhood for a Black family or two who would let them change clothes and perhaps have a room for the night.

Recalling this experience as well as others like it led Brooks one day to tell a white sportswriter that "Being a Negro is an interesting life because every morning he wakes up to find a challenge staring him in the face."

The 1956 baseball season proved an impressive one for Brooks. He was on a winning streak. By the time he finished his seventh straight win, he had pitched in twelve games where he started nine and pitched three completed ones. The Redlegs had not lost a single game that Brooks started. After seven straight wins, Brooks had gone 72 and 2/3 innings, giving up 68 hits and 32 runs, with only 25 of them earned. Brooks also walked 33 players and struck out 25 of them. That year one of the highlights of baseball was on June 22nd, when the Dodgers met the Reds at Ebbets Field in Brooklyn, New York. Brooks pitched a "two-hitter" and the Reds romped the Dodgers 6-0. Carl Furillo and Jackie Robinson were the only Dodgers to break Brooks' pitching magic. Furillo, a right fielder for the Dodgers, hit a single in the 5th inning. In the 8th inning, Jackie Robinson came up to bat. A scene of the past flashed through Brooks' mind as he remembered pitching for St. Louis and striking Jackie out with a curve ball. Brooks knew not to throw that pitch again. So, instead of throwing a curve ball, he opted to throw a screwball, or fade-away pitch, that he had learned when he was under the tutelage of major league Cardinals' coach, Bill Posedel, a former pitcher for the Brooklyn Dodgers and Boston Braves. Jackie cracked a double, but no players made it to home plate.

Brooks called Reds' catcher, Ed Bailey, halfway to the mound while a left-handed batter stood in the box anxiously awaiting the signal.

"What's the pitch?" asked Ed.

"Well, Bailey," Brooks said, "If Jackie tries to break for the plate, I'll pitch out so you can tag him."

"Got it," Ed said walking back to his position.

Brooks struck out the batter and the Reds held off the Dodgers from breaking any runs to home base. By the end of the 9th inning, Brooks had won his 9th straight game of the season. Gabe Paul's trade of Jackie Collum to acquire Brooks was paying off for the Redlegs. By mid season, Brooks had twice whipped the Brooklyn Dodgers, the Chicago Cubs, the Philadelphia Phillies, and the Milwaukee Braves. After one of the Milwaukee games, Brooks spent some time with Jim Pendleton, who played for the Braves. They talked about their experiences playing baseball before they got into the major leagues. Jim described a baseball game he played in Iwo Jima, and they discovered that he and Brooks had met on a military plane en route back to Guam after the game. Neither had thought then that years later they would meet each other again and both be playing major league baseball.

Brooks was considered the "winningest" pitcher in the National League and one of the top pitchers. By his tenth win, against the Pittsburgh Pirates, the Redlegs became top contenders in the pennant race for the first time in more than ten years. They were only one-half game short of first place in the National League. As a result of his outstanding performance, Brooks received a telegram on July 2, 1956, at the Black-owned and operated Manse Hotel in Cincinnati, where he stayed when playing in Cincinnati. From Warren C. Giles, President of the National League, it read, "YOU HAVE BEEN SELECTED AS A MEMBER OF THE NATIONAL LEAGUE ALL STAR TEAM AND I EXTEND MY SINCERE CONGRATULATIONS. YOU HAVE EARNED AND DESERVE THIS RECOGNITION. THE NATIONAL LEAGUE HAS WON FIVE OF THE LAST SIX ALL STAR GAMES AND ARE SURE YOU WILL HELP US ADD ANOTHER VICTORY IN WASHINGTON ON JULY TENTH."

This wasn't the only congratulatory telegram he received. On the morning of the All Star game, he was pleasantly surprised to hear from his former Caguas manager, Mickey Owen. Mickey wished him good luck, saying, "It's been a long hard pull from Caguas to the top, but you made it." Mickey's message especially touched Brooks' heart because he remained deeply grateful for Mickey's guidance.

The All Star game was played in Washington, D.C. at Griffith Stadium with 28,843 fans in attendance. At the time, the fans could choose the players to be the starting eight for the All Star game. However, the league manager was the one who chose the pitcher. Many fans wanted Brooks to take the mound, but he made it only to warming up in the bullpen. Of the twenty-six players making up the squads for both leagues, nine from the National League did not play and five from the American League did not. Still, the players felt it was an honor just to be on the 1956 All Star team. (The National League won the game for the sixth time with a score of 7-3; there was no Most Valuable Player Award until the year 1962.)

Though Brooks knew that there was a possibility that he would not pitch in the All Star game, he was somewhat disappointed that he didn't get a taste of the mound. But this letdown didn't get in the way of his winning streak. On July 17, he snagged his thirteenth straight win by beating the Brooklyn Dodgers at Crosley Field, with a score of 4-3. Brooks was now edging closer to the goal of a pitcher's dream . . . to win twenty games in a season. Could he tie or break Ewell Blackwell's record of sixteen straight wins for the Redlegs in 1947? Or could he equal or surpass an all-time major league record of nineteen straight wins set by Rube Marquard of the New York Giants, who in 1912 had tied Giants pitcher, Tim Keefe's record of 1888? The talk of Brooks' possible achievement buzzed like a swarm of bees in baseball clubhouses and amongst the fans.

On July 21st, the Redlegs played the Pittsburgh Pirates at Crosley Field. Brooks gave up three hits, two singles and a double in the first two innings, with the Pirates scoring a run in the first inning. After that, only one Pirate made it as far as second base. Brooks then proceeded to hold the Pirates hitless for the next six innings. During the third inning, with only one out, Brooks and the Redlegs' second baseman hit successive doubles giving Cincinnati a 2-1 lead over Pittsburgh. In the fourth frame, a Redlegs shortstop hit the ball, but it ended up in a second base force out. However, Frank Robinson was on third base and successfully made it home. The run gave the Redlegs a 3-1 lead that they were able to hold as they entered into the ninth inning.

The noise of the crowd boomed throughout the stadium; while Brooks stood motionless on the mound, holding his ball and mitt behind his back, waiting for the next batter. Careful not to let his mind drift into the stands with the fans, he focused on outsmarting the batter. So far, he had not been threatened in the past six innings, but he knew that on any given day anything could happen. Within a split second after starting his windup, he released a slider that whisked across the plate so fast that it startled the outfielder who was up to bat.

"Strike," yelled the umpire.

Holding the bat and stretching his arms, the outfielder took a couple of long breaths to help control his timing.

Positioning himself again, he lunged forward at the next fastball and smacked a single. A Redleg rally suddenly swept the field. The Redlegs fans could taste victory but wanted to ensure it. The Pirates' first baseman carefully stood in the batting box with hopes of picking up the signal. Just for an instant, the batter took his eyes off the ball and glanced over at the first baseman. Brooks seized the opportunity and hurled a "cut" fastball. Without swinging, the Pirate held onto the bat and jumped behind the plate to move out of the way.

"Ball one," said the umpire.

The batter readied himself for another 90 miles-an-hour fastball, but Brooks tricked him and threw a circular change-up. Barely getting a piece of it, the batter hit a fly ball.

"Out!" yelled the umpire.

The Pirates' third baseman came to the plate. Brooks threw a sinker.

"Ball One," yelled the umpire.

Brooks threw another sinker. The batter managed to hit a line drive and made it safely to first base. Two hitters were now on base and the Pirate fans went wild. Right fielder Roberto Clemente approached the batting box. Brooks definitely did not want the bases to become loaded nor did he want any more runs. He knew from past experience with the Pirates that Clemente hated the outside breaking pitch but had learned how to hit it. Taking his chances, Brooks threw the ball. Clemente swung and missed.

"Strike," yelled the umpire.

Brooks threw another one.

"Strike Two."

Clemente wiped the sweat from his face. To relax himself, he rolled his head a couple of times and stretched his aching back. Positioning himself once more, he steadied his gaze on the ball. Brooks, going for an outside curve, hurled the ball. It raced through the air at lightning speed but never broke to the outside. Instead, it remained in hang-time over the heart of the plate. Brooks had gotten Clemente out with low balls before, but this time, the ball had slipped from his hand on the release and gone high. Clemente loved high balls, and the ball landed right where he wanted it. He hammered the ball over the inner fence in right field, a three-run homer. Brooks stood in disbelief. The Redlegs and their fans gasped, stunned as if the wind had been knocked out of them. The Pirates' fans erupted in hysterical glee; their team was now in the lead with a score of 4-3. Brooks retired the next two batters, but he had a gut feeling that his thirteen game winning streak had come to an end. He was soon proven right. With some great relief pitching by Pirate Roy Face, the Redlegs just couldn't recover and the Pirates' lead held. Brooks felt that he had pitched a good game, so except for wishing the outcome had been different, he had no regrets. He shook off the defeat and immediately started concentrating on capturing twenty wins for the season. In spite of the loss, Brooks' thirteen straight games winning streak still stands in second place in the records of the Reds' ball club.

Redlegs' fans in Brooks' hometown of Springfield and elsewhere in the vicinity wanted to do something special to honor their hero after Brooks had won his twelfth straight game. Since a couple of other players, Wally Post and Walter Alston, had been previously honored at a Redlegs' game by their relatives, friends, and/or hometown, it was suggested that Springfield sponsor a "Haddix-Lawrence Day." Harvey Haddix, a pitcher for the Philadelphia Phillies and like Brooks raised in Clark County, was living in Springfield. Since the Redlegs were scheduled to play a doubleheader against the Phillies at Crosley Field on August 26, 1956, Springfield's general manager, Harold Cheek, and the Chamber of Commerce spearheaded a Haddix-Lawrence Day. Both major league hurlers were slated to gather at home plate with their wives and parents and be celebrated as "best in the game" during the pre-game festivities. The Chamber of Commerce established two committees to organize voluntary gift donations for both ball players. One committee collected cash to purchase U.S. Savings Bonds while the other committee collected merchandise gifts. Cost for the game was five bucks which included a round-trip train ride from Springfield and reserve seats at the ballpark. The train was scheduled to leave the Pennsylavania RailRoad Yard on Springfield's South Limestone Street at 9:30 a.m. and return one hour after the last ball game, arriving after 7:30 p.m. The Chamber of Commerce secured almost 2,000 seats for the event, but close to 3,000 city and county fans, including little leaguers in uniform, attended the game. A grand total of 28,361 fans turned out to pay tribute at Crosley Field. The Redlegs won the opener of the doubleheader 10-5, contributing to Brooks' sixteenth win of the season. (But in the nightcap, the Phillies defeated the Redlegs with a score of 11-4.)

On the first of September, the Redlegs defeated the Chicago Cubs once more, and Brooks captured his seventeenth win of the season. At one point, as the game became more intense, the Cubs' pitcher, "Sad" Sam Jones, threw a temper tantrum, protesting to the umpire that Brooks was intentionally throwing the ball at him. Brooks didn't say a word and looked at Sam as if he was crazy. Frustrated, the umpire, Augie Donatelli, called Red's manager, George "Birdie" Tedbetts, over to home plate. Sam stood at home base and with his right hand kept swinging the bat low, while he waited for the game to continue.

"Look," Augie said, and pointed to Sam and Brooks, "I warned those two in an earlier inning about throwing high pitches. Sam's been throwing high pitches and has already hit the backstop. So, what's Lawrence gonna do?"

Standing with both hands on his hips, Birdie looked Augie square in the eyes and gave him a sharp reply. "I don't know," he said. "But he won't kill him."

Augie turned around facing Brooks and Sam. Throwing his hands up in disgust he roared, "Play ball."

Brooks threw a slider. Sam swung and missed.

"Strike three," called the umpire.

Sam scuffed off the field and Brooks proceeded to nab a 7-3 win.

On September 15th, the Redlegs battled the Pirates in Pittsburgh. On a run during the second inning, Brooks slid to home plate and scored. The 6-4 win over the Pirates advanced Brooks to his nineteenth win. Now the heat was really on, and Birdie was in a dilemma: It is extremely difficult for a pitcher to win twenty games in a season, and for a black man to achieve this feat was rarely heard of. Many people cheered Brooks as he eased closer to twenty wins, but there were ball players, baseball associates and baseball lovers who were not ready for such an achievement by Brooks Lawrence to become part of baseball history.

Brooks had always credited Birdie for his role in Brooks' seasonal success. He felt that Birdie let him pitch the way he wanted to and helped him believe in himself again. By the same token, Birdie knew that the Redlegs had a very good chance to win the pennant and needed Brooks to help them do it. But Birdie couldn't handle the pressure from the prevailing resistance to Brooks' impending achievement. Because of the times and his own deep-rooted issues, he didn't want to take the risk. He just couldn't let it happen. He chose not to allow Brooks to pitch.

Inevitably, Birdie's decision was questioned by many Redlegs' fans. Friends and acquaintances of the Lawrence family asked Brooks' wife, parents and siblings when was Brooks going to pitch. But they didn't know any more than the fans. Sometimes when the townsfolk commented that Birdie's decision just wasn't right, the family agreed. But Brooks still did not get to play.

The season was in its final two weeks when Brooks began to seriously wonder if he would get another start. He finally approached Birdie at Shibe Park in Philadelphia, just before a game with the Phillies.

"Hey, Birdie," Brooks said. "What happened to my turn? When do I start?"

Birdie acted as if he hadn't heard him.

"When do I start?" Brooks repeated. The firmness of his voice clearly showed he would not be ignored.

Birdie knew this day was inevitable, and he had prepared himself a few days earlier. He took a deep breath, and replied, "You won't get to start. There's no way that I'm going to let you win twenty games on my watch."

Brooks knew immediately what Birdie meant. He knew that once again he was a victim of bigotry and racism. There was nothing he could do against it, though he vowed never to embrace it. So as a result of Birdie's decision, Brooks didn't pitch another game for the rest of the season. Despite this great setback, 1956 was the best season of his career; he finished with a 19-10 record. However, Birdie's judgment call crippled the Redlegs' chances of grabbing the pennant; they ended up in third place.

No matter how many storms showered upon Brooks, he remained always a gentleman. He let the raindrops roll off of him and never dwelt on the negative. He always redirected his energies in a positive and productive manner. Thus, the following year, 1957, he finished the season with 16 wins and 13 losses. In 1958, he ended the season with a record of 8-13. In 1959 and 1960, his record was 7-12 and 1-0, respectively.

Early one morning near the end of the 1958 season, on an off day for the Reds, Brooks drove out to Crosley Field to do some "soul searching." He walked onto the playing field, making sure that he didn't step on the foul line, which in baseball circles was bad luck. Standing on the pitcher's mound he invited the silent welcome of the field to soothe his thoughts. Now thirty-three years old, he knew that time was catching up with his arm. At best, he would have a couple of more years left in the big leagues. But more importantly, he had a strong feeling that in 1959 he would probably do mostly relief pitching and after the 1960 season it was likely that he would no longer wear number 46.

"What will I do next?" he wondered. He recalled the time when his hero, Jackie Robinson, crossed the color line and came to play in Cincinnati. He looked at the empty stands where once along with droves of other Black Americans he'd waited to see Jackie play that May 13th day of Jackie's rookie year. Those fans had traveled in trains, buses and cars from the South, from nearby states and, of course, from the greater Cincinnati area. And because of Jackie's courage, they were able to dream, once more of the possibilities.

In Brooks' eyes, Jackie was the "epitome of a man" because even though the pressure on Jackie was monumental, he maintained balance. When Brooks and Jackie had their friendly talks after a game, they talked about many things, including societal injustice, civil rights and social change. Often Jackie did more of the talking and Brooks just listened, sometimes asking a question but mostly absorbing Jackie's viewpoint. Jackie said people should be judged on merit and not on the color of their skin. Jackie had so believed in equality for everyone that at one time he suggested to the sports media, businessmen, and others that Brooks should become the first Black manager of an organized ball club. He said no one in major league baseball was more qualified for a managerial duty than Brooks, who had intelligence, a strong work ethic and a thorough knowledge of the game. Jackie said Brooks worked well with others, and he was genuine.

Brooks looked up at the stands again and then at the home plate. How many pitches had he thrown across there? It had felt so good to hurl those balls to some of the best ball players in the world. *"It has been a long haul,"* he reflected. *"The journey to the top has not been easy."* That's when he suddenly remembered what of one of his minor league coaches, once said to him during a practice session. "You're good," the man had said. "You're real good, but you'll never make it," he said, with the self-satisfied smirk of a small-mind, "because I'll see to it that you don't."

Brooks smiled, remembering that prediction. Because it reminded him of the sweet memory of a particular major league game. Brooks had made his first hit and was rounding the bases to stop on third. He looked at the opposing team's third base coach and smiled, his eyes gleaming in triumph. When the next batter slugged the ball, Brooks, ready to run home, couldn't resist. The third base coach was his old minor league coach with the mean-spirited prediction. As he dashed off the base for home plate, he winked at the man and said, "I made it." Dodging the catcher, he slid for home.

"Safe," yelled the umpire.

He did make it!

And if a man

Can live his dream

Despite his creed or race

Then baseball is the heart of my home

And I have found my place.

*(**My Place** by Cheryl D. Lyons)*

Extra Inning

Brooks' life scored all the way around. In his seven-year major league career, he played in 275 games and compiled a lifetime pitching record of 69 wins and 62 losses with a 4.25 ERA (Earned Run Average.) In later years, he was inducted into the Cincinnati Reds Hall of Fame, the Ohio Baseball Hall of Fame and the Springfield South High School Athletic Hall of Fame.

Although Brooks never became the first black manager, as Jackie Robinson had recommended, the many firsts in his life include:

> The 1st Black Quarterback at Keifer Jr. High and Springfield South High Schools
>
> The 1st Black Man in the Ohio-Indiana Class D League
>
> One of the 1st two Black Men with the Columbus, Ohio Redbirds AAA League
>
> One of the 1st two Black Men with the St. Louis Cardinals
>
> The 1st Black Man on the Cincinnati Reds Administration
>
> The 1st Black Man inducted into the Cincinnati Reds Hall of Fame
>
> The 1st Black Baseball Coach at Wilmington College in Wilmington, Ohio, and
>
> The 1st Black Baseball Player at Miami University in Oxford, Ohio.

Lightning Source UK Ltd.
Milton Keynes UK
UKHW011848140121
377077UK00008B/565/J

9 781413 477511